# IT'S ONLY
# FISHING

*Tales of Alaska, fly fishing, and young adulthood*

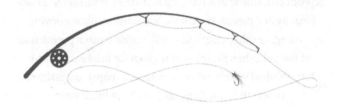

## JOSEPH JACKSON

Epicenter Press Inc.
Alaska Book Adventures™

Kenmore, WA

6524 NE 181st St., Suite 2, Kenmore, WA 98028

Epicenter Press is a regional press publishing nonfiction
books about the arts, history, environment, and diverse
cultures and lifestyles of Alaska and the Pacific Northwest.
For more information, visit www.EpicenterPress.com

It's Only Fishing
Copyright © 2023 by Joseph Jackson

*Cover and author photos: Emelia Jackson*
*Cover design: Scott Book*
*Interior design: Melissa Vail Coffman*

ISBN: 978-1-684920-39-6 (Trade Paperback)
ISBN: 978-1-684920-40-2 (Ebook)

Produced in the United States of America

*To Dad and Pops, for showing me how.*
*To Mom and Emelia, for letting me go.*
*And to Hank, for being the first to accompany me.*

*"You could say the same thing about fishing that they say about baseball: that it takes an adult to play the game well, but it takes a kid to think it's important."*

—John Gierach

# INTRODUCTION

T HE BEST COMPLIMENT I'VE EVER RECEIVED is that I might spend a little too much time fishing.

To the people delivering such statements, or admonishments, it *is* only fishing; a pastime that, aside from being one that's possible to spend too much time on in the first place, can also be described as 'silly,' 'boring,' and/or occasionally 'pointless.' I have to cede that this is true, at least from the outside looking in, but at the same time, I am compelled to point out that not only can you describe a good many careers using these same three descriptors, but just because something is 'pointless' does not mean that it's not worth doing.

To me, fishing is everything that matters. It's the child's joy of being hoodwinked. It's grasping at the smoke of understanding our world. It's making the impossible attempt—in the same way people shoot for love, success, happiness—to capture pinpricks of light and memory set against a stage of water, flowing or otherwise. Or maybe it's none of that. Maybe it *is* just silly, boring, and pointless.

But what isn't?

OVER MY TWENTY YEARS OF FOLLOWING WATER, I've come to the belief that you can learn something each time you go fishing. That something might be practical, such as where the trout hide in a given logjam on a full-sunny day of a new moon, or it might be of the metaphysical, such as how the world came into being and your ultimate purpose on its soil. It might be something stupid like finally remembering where you left that set of drill bits. In any case, you come away with *something*, and that something either fades off into the ether as soon as you get back into the truck, or it floats through your mind for days afterward until it spins itself into meaning (or it might just fade off into the ether anyway, albeit a bit later).

Armed with this theory, I set forth into 2020 with a goal: I would write an essay—totally variable in length and purpose— for each fishing trip I took. Some of the smaller outings I would combine into one piece of perhaps a few paragraphs, while more complex trips could go on for pages. All these stories would be snipped and edited to the point they weren't complete slop, and, indeed, some entire pieces have been left out because they were just that.

The larger decision was mostly in the interest of keeping track of what I'd done, in the same way that people devote themselves to taking photos or recording videos. I prefer to try and capture my world with the written word. I didn't think the experience would make me a better angler (though maybe a more observant one), and I certainly didn't think it would make me a more intelligent or philosophical member of the human race. I just figured it would be fun to pull out of a drawer in a couple of decades and see what the heck I did with myself back in the day.

Little did I know, when I set this goal, what the fishing season would hold. That was part of the fun: I would live out the narrative as it unfolded. But I don't even think a novelist could've plotted something as wild as 2020.

As I was planning the season (say January or February), I had an embarrassment of options being that I call Alaska home year-round. There were the usual haunts to return to, the new species or larger specimens to check off, the rumored creeks that I'd been wanting to fish but hadn't, and, in general, all the antsy plans that tend to build up over our long winters in between set-lining for burbot or hunting snowshoe hares. Since I'm a devoted fly angler 99% of the time, there was also all this hand-tied work arranged in my fly boxes practically shouting to be used.

By March, just as I was starting to become positively giddy at the prospect of having a rod back in my hands, things turned sideways. I feel no need to explain the situation any more than that; you, dear reader, have your own stark memories of just what 'sideways' meant.

For me, the coronavirus pandemic meant that the original three days I'd planned to spend with my wife, Emmie, in Juneau (where she was working at the time) turned into three weeks; and that by the time we were able to move her out of there, we had to receive special permission from the Canadian government to drive through the border at Haines. It also meant that my job became not only totally online, but also totally vital to a steadily growing mob of people. (I was an educational video producer for the University of Alaska Fairbanks. When everyone realized that they'd have to deliver their courses via the internet, my inbox exploded and I reached my voicemail storage quota—neither of which I success-fully managed to clear, by the way). The ensuing summer left me in a sort of daze.

2020 was my best fishing season yet, and, oddly enough, a perfect stage against which to let my story unfold. Somehow, things just worked out, and I spent more time fishing than I did any other year. Most of it probably had to do with the fact that teleworking is just a perfect excuse to fish on weekdays, but a lot of it (and now we're straying into sappy territory) was because I needed fishing more than I ever have. Aside from my wife and my cat, really, the cork of a fly rod and the rhythmic clack of my vest became my constants through all manner of change: a pandemic, a planned but drastic career shift in which I dropped my salaried media position for an unpaid teaching internship, a series of frantic moves between three homes, and the general angst of young adulthood. Fishing had been steadily working its way into my soul—like a tenacious parasite—since I was old enough to do it, but in a year when I was stuck between occupations and not sure of what else I could be, I became a fisherman. What follows are my attempts to explain why that didn't disappoint me.

FISHING IS THE ONLY THING THAT has brought me to a riverbank at daybreak, when I can feel the mist like cashmere on my skin and imagine a salmon fighting against the weight of glaciers a hundred miles from where my feet are planted. It's the only thing that's left me standing on a lakeshore at midnight, my mind all at once desolate and bursting, staring at a surface as calm as cellophane until a lone beaver, uninterested in me, glides by. Fishing is one of a select number of things that make me feel lucky; aware of my own lungs and the throbbing songs of boreal owls, aware of my own ability to decide between what is productive and what is pointless, and then to choose the latter. It's my constant through evolution—then, now, and tomorrow—and though my words won't ever repay nor do justice to anything that's put me here, as Ken Marsh once said in his book *Breakfast at Trout's Place*, "words for now will have to do."

When I look fifty years into the future, I see either an old man with a dog at heel and a shaft of bamboo in his hand, or a flotsam of ashes spin drifting down a lonely stream toward the sea. In either case, I hope they all turn to each other at my funeral and begin whispering amongst themselves. It'll be hushed at first until they realize that I'm not around and they can say whatever they want to.

"He was a good guy," they'll proclaim, a little louder, and maybe a few will believe it. "But he might've spent just a *little* too much time fishing."

# ONE: GOOD NEWS

THE BEGINNING OF FISHING SEASON IS ALWAYS a bit difficult to believe in Interior Alaska. We've been watching the snow melt and the days lengthen for weeks; we've been wondering when the ice will go out, when the grayling will start moving in to spawn, when the turbid flows will thin to a surge that's not totally insane to plop a nymph into. This progression is neither quick nor predictable. Some years it will be the second week of May. Other years it will be at the tail end of April.

It's not as though I'm *not* fishing one day and the next day I am. It's more like I hear the woody songs of sandhill cranes and start to see more and more pintails arrive in the melt ponds and I think, "Man, I wonder if it's too early, but what-the-hell let's try it anyway." I get up before dawn and make the coffee, and I try not to think of it as 'fishing coffee' because I still don't know if that's what it is yet. And then, before I know it or even have time to commemorate it, I flip a U-turn across the bridge because, by God, the river's open. I'm in waders and the fly rod is loading on the backcast and sure it's a little clunky, but it's just like riding a bike.

In 2020, the thresholds of spring were more ambiguous than normal. Toward mid-March, just when I was starting to kick the fly-tying into gear and think about sea-run cutthroats along the coast, a little virus from Wuhan, China started popping up on the news. I didn't think too much about it. I was more worried if the fly shop would carry Mylar in the right thickness and shade of green. Then that little virus started spreading.

Before I knew it, my plans for some early-bird saltwater fishing were dashed and we were homebound for five weeks, reduced to atoms in the nexus of a global pandemic. Social-distancing, self-quarantine, watch-the-toilet-paper-supply and all that rot. Granted, I had some heroic bouts of fly-tying and got a bunch of Gierach read in those days, but even so, one can't stave off the shack nasties forever.

My wife, Emmie, and I had had plans to move from Fairbanks to Anchorage in late summer for the high-school teaching internship I'd be beginning down there. But with the world on the brink of collapse, and the city of Fairbanks feeling like a toxic balloon about to pop, we packed up and departed a little early—the first of April, as I recall. We retreated south to her parents' farm in the Copper River valley (I swear we were invited), and we ended up staying for the better part of five months.

All of this, it would turn out, made for a lovely spring. After the snow began to melt, I crept across an open hayfield to get within photo range of a bevy of trumpeter swans. I watched the runoff churn into the culvert below the driveway and dared to wonder if the nearby creeks were starting to do the same, even though I knew it was way too early. When it comes to fishing, I always jump the gun.

Sometimes it doesn't hurt to wish for good news, though.

THE PROBLEM WITH SPRING FISHING is that it's easy to be overzealous. I mean, here I am not having touched a fly rod since October.

My fly boxes are full to bursting with the experiments and the standbys. There aren't many fish around yet, and the high flows are carrying and concealing a wickerwork of snags just waiting to swallow all that work. But I don't care. It's like what Dad says: "A fool and his money are soon parted." Five casts and I've lost two flies; one's in the tree behind me and the other I dropped in the water because my hands were shaking so bad with the cold. Oh well. Easy come, easy go. You can really go through that new spool of tippet this way, too.

I try to refrain from doing it all again this year. Just be patient, I chide. The fish will be around in mid-May. Just wait out the runoff, wait out the spawn, and come to it gently.

By the last week of April, though, the snow was really gone, and the sandhill cranes had started landing with some regularity. I'd even seen a pintail drake arrive, his chocolate-colored head swiveling like a periscope, his tail sharp as a dart. I started thinking about a trip north to Fairbanks, one I could rationalize as a mail-check and grocery-run, but one that would serve as an invaluable scouting expedition, too. I'd pass four premiere grayling streams on the way, and even if it was taboo to check this early, that was all right because I wasn't going solely to *fish*.

Off I went at four the next morning, sipping coffee from the fishing thermos but refusing to think of it as fishing coffee. That would've really jinxed it.

In a predawn gloom as soft as a Rusty Heurlin painting, I turned down onto the campground road that would take me across stream number one. In the summertime, this creek crawls beneath white-spruce and alder, but now it's surging and frothing beneath the bridge like the first release of irrigation water at lower latitudes. I'm sure a grayling could find a Prince nymph or a stonefly if you cast it into the right place, though it could just as easily turn into one of those scenarios where I lose a weekend's worth of tying.

I press on, listening to Tom Rosenbauer talk about fishing hatches (the kind I won't see until June), and pass stream number two. Located in a mountain pass, the place is still covered in two feet of snow, but the river cuts through it like a vein of silver in quartz. In July, the place will be crammed with motorhomes from Ohio wanting to see the spawning sockeyes (though maybe not, if travel restrictions persist), but right now it's dead.

The third creek turns out to be locked in ice, then an hour later, I resolve to save the fourth (and likeliest) stream for the return journey. I'll try and hit it at a little past noon, when, historically, I've seen mayflies hatch as early as the 3rd of May.

In Fairbanks I run my errands with the freneticism of a squirrel stocking his midden. I get the check engine light inspected (probably a short in the wiring), I buy lumber at Home Depot for a construction project I've been putting off, then I pay a visit to Reed Morisky, (always *Mr.* Morisky to me), who has to be *the* Arctic grayling aficionado and someone who's as antsy as I am to get on some fish. Years ago, I produced a short documentary about his fly-fishing career, and I was currently in the early stages of writing his outdoor biography. That man has had a life, let me tell you. Today he's saved a box of old fishing magazines for me that's about as heavy as an engine block. We kick at the gravel in his driveway and talk about the news in our respective worlds and how crazy things have been with the coronavirus and being homebound. He tells me he ran up the Nenana River the day before to check on his pair of cabins up there. The report:

"The river was open, but I didn't see any grayling."

Not the best news, but not the worst news either. He tells me he's thinking about going down to "the Clearwater" in the next few days, just to see if there's anything around.

"That's where I'm headed this afternoon," I say. The fourth stream on my list. "I'll let you know if it's any good."

We both agree that there have just *got* to be fish in there. Perhaps our combined wishful thinking will conjure up some grayling.

I make the grocery and mail runs I said I was going to make, then I blow off a virtual meeting for work on the grounds that 'I'm editing. Do not disturb.' That's usually a good enough reason for a video editor to make people leave you alone.

By noon I'm back on the road, headed the opposite direction I just came all four-and-a-half hours for. As I near the Clearwater, a quick flurry of snow riddles the sky, and then it's right back to postcard blue. I pull into the campground and try to remember the ratio that Tom Rosenbauer suggested on a dry-fly leader to get it to turn over correctly. My heart does a little skip when I see I'm the only one here, but then again, this is a full month earlier than most people dare to arrive. Below, the river looks like obsidian. Cold and biting even from the comfort of a heated seat. I tie up slowly next to the truck—patience, kid—then I slip into the waders and hardly dare to wonder if this will be it . . . the *first* time of the year . . .

I stumble down to the water like a new calf. The trail is crusted over in a good foot of ice yet, but the river is chuckling, and a pair of gulls are bobbing like sloops at harbor. Into the water, my boots heavy. Weight around my ankles, then my calves, the first seeps through the hole I couldn't quite patch. Now cold. Now casting.

I knock some rust off the hinges and humble myself with a few windknots. It's not five minutes before a blizzard of what looks like Styrofoam pellets starts dumping from clouds as thick as cast-iron. It gets down the back of my hood and I seize up and the cold starts coming in from everywhere; the spring-water crawling up my leg, the air of late April just a degree above freezing, the sharp pings of snow on my hands, my neck, my nose. But hey, I'm fishing. I've waited *months* for this, even if I'm absurdly early once again.

*I'm fishing.*

And then, magically, the grayling are here with me. Rising, flipping. It's like I'm surrounded by a pod of whales in the open ocean, trying to guess where the next will surface, my head snapping to the breaches of others. I make a flurry of casts into fish that know my game.

Flotillas of mayflies and caddis roll by, wings in full canvas, and I have an imitation of the right color but just a tad too big. My fingers are useless already as I struggle to change the fly. I fan-cast to the swirls of feeding fish, overwhelmed by the sheer number, stricken with inaction. They ignore me. Another fly-change. It's so cold that I drop the old one and let it float away—easy come easy go—and then I try feeding a downstream cast. Usually, these Arctic rogues don't take you to school but they sure are now.

All I want is that moment. The cosmic half-second where the water boils right where you know your fly is, the instinct coded in your proteins as you lift and feel the rod bend against something as vital as you are. A good life is a chain of these moments where you reach out and touch something beyond yourself. They can be separated by weeks, months, years, but they come just often enough to keep you coming back. Enough to keep you impatient for the next.

That moment doesn't come for me. Not today. I lose a fly in the spruce behind me and drop another one. Eventually the snow stops but so do the rising fish, and the only remnants of this little miracle I've witnessed are some wayward caddisflies that I scoop up and commit to memory for replication at the vice tomorrow—tonight, even. I'm not one to admit defeat too often, but it seems to me that patience in this scenario is knowing when to fold 'em.

On the way back to the truck I try and justify it all. Fishermen only get introspective when they haven't caught anything. But in the same instant that I want to feel disappointed, inadequate, even, I realize that just seeing the somersaulting shapes of grayling has lit an old fire; the one I haven't felt since last fall. Before I know it, I'm reeling with excitement and the joy of looking ahead. Things can only get better from here.

I crunch out of the campground and onto the main road again, headed west into the blizzard that seems to be following me. I sip tepid coffee—fishing coffee, you bet—and listen to the heater and the whir of quick tires. On the shoulder I stop and pull out my phone and shoot a text to Mr. Morisky.

Plenty of rising grayling in the Clearwater. Hatches of #14-16 gray caddisflies and #14 mayflies.

Five minutes down the road, my phone buzzes with a reply: Best news I've heard in a long time.

# TWO: QUESTIONS

I'M STANDING IN WATER THAT'S UP to my crotch, which is how I discover there's a hole in my waders near the belt. Within seconds my right leg is soaked to the hilt, though I hardly notice. My attention is puppeted by the tiny little dry fly riding the surface, bobbing gently over ripples formed by the island break below me. It's right where it should be, right where the grayling rose ten seconds ago, and it should be any moment, any moment at all . . .

The rise is tragically short when it comes, though I'm not sure I could handle such elation in perpetuity. I lift, as gently as I can, and feel the rioting tugs of a creature stunned by the unfamiliar. A minute later I draw a long Arctic grayling into the net, his scales radiating every color of Alaska from gunmetal to rosehip red to forget-me-not blue. I let him go quickly out of the selfish motivation to get back to casting, and the next drift might have been a mirror image of the first. Another fish takes but I miss it.

Mankind knows no question greater than looking at a river and wondering what's beneath its musical creases. From the swirls and dimples and currents etching themselves on the surface, one can extrapolate what is happening underneath—the shape of the bottom, the drawstrings of hidden currents and undertow, the character of fish, crustaceans, and aquatic insects that might live there. The allure is that even in this desperate guessing we never know. The river is movingly close yet unattainably far; it is so near our understanding that we can almost taste it—like we've tasted lunar rocks—yet it bears and undergoes complexities that we will never understand.

While far from coughing up answers, angling gives a chance to take the pulse of such an unknown. When you cast a hook and line, it falls outward in the shape of a question mark, and success gives a fleeting elation of understanding, of belonging, of a small clue to this gargantuan mudball made known just for us. Subsurface fishing remains mysterious until the moment the fish is landed; brought to hand, studied, identified, and either released with a gentle whorl or unceremoniously clonked on the head and thrown on a stringer. Surface fishing, more specifically *dry-fly fishing*, is slightly more immediate in its validation.

I know there are grayling here; I *know* that they arrive in late April (some of those too young to spawn will arrive even earlier); I know the water trickles up from aquifers and hosts stupendous hatches of caddisflies and mayflies alike, and I know that between noon and 3 p.m., said hatch is underway and fish rise by the dozens beneath a particular campground in Interior Alaska. It might appear that I know much about this gentle river and its gentle fish, but each outing and drift with a dry fly suggests the opposite.

Each porpoising rise, either accompanied by a bewildered fight or a clean miss, sends me riding on the most ephemeral of druglike highs. Suddenly, magically, I'm enlightened. The fish is netted, and I stand there wondering why—if the evolutionary function of life is simply to survive—God made some things so pretty, moreover the reptilian clade of fishes. From above, Arctic grayling don't look much different than the mottling of a river surface, which you can look down on from the campground without getting your feet wet.

But viewed from the side, the small reward that anglers receive, they burst in neon colors as vivid as wildflowers, painted to draw mates in their ritualistic procreation of spring. Why, then, do they retain these colors through the year? Fish become living, breathing, pulsating questions, made known by a simple bend of metal with a few wraps of musk-ox wool and a stack of deer hair. They leap with all the magnificence of shooting stars. You release them and it is then you realize that you don't know anything. What the river has lent it has now taken back.

Finally, I'm shaking so bad with cold and excitement that I can't connect my tippet to a fly to save my life, and I slosh back up to the campground and dump the water from my waders. As I prepare to depart, I give one last look to the sweeping gleam of the river, where the hatch is over, the surface is quiet, and the pools look empty.

# THREE: TERNS OF FATE

LOOKING SOUTH THROUGH THE SKELETAL BRANCHES of willow, you watch the sky crawl closer and closer. It's heavy with moisture and bound to be snow at this elevation, but you pull out the rain jacket and bear it. You've told yourself you're going fishing, and such a commitment transcends any worldly trouble. To your right the creek runs heavy with melted avalanches and glacial waste; further still in that direction, the mountains of the Alaska Range rise unseen to be eaten by fog. To your backside a U-Haul roars by, kicking up spray like the debris behind asteroids. Its driver is wondering just what you're doing out here in the rain with a fly rod and a pair of hip boots. You might ask yourself the same, but you don't. Some questions are best unasked.

You lock the truck, more a mechanized habit than any concern of theft, and you think about what the lake inlet will look like, how deep the snow will be, if you'll *finally* hook up to one of those mackinaws of lore. Off you go whistling through the tundra-bush.

YOU'VE FISHED IN HIGHER PLACES BEFORE, but here on this bench between the Pacific and the tallest mountains in North America, it sure doesn't feel like it. The land is carpeted in lean desolation; brittle grasses and sedges, dwarf birch and willow, thirsty white spruce clinging to life like an old man in the terminal ward. Everything here feels ancient and anonymous. You remain silent, bound within invisible reverence for the place, smelling its clean air, watching the hills fold over themselves for as far as you can see. It's around then that you decide this land might just go on forever, and while one part of you yearns to see more of it, the other hopes that no one does.

Knee-deep snow on the trail. You brought the hip boots for wading in water, but they shield the snow with equal effect. You follow the tracks of a wayward fox, you see where he stopped to pee, and you know it's a he because you can see three tracks straddling this blueberry bush and you can imagine the fourth lifted high in salute. You might crack a grin at the simplicity of his world, but then you remind yourself to get moving. This lake is but a stop on the journey, and you still have two hundred miles to drive after this.

The creek hurries when you finally intercept it on the trail, and you follow along its lip. Now at the inlet, where the flow forks, you know you must cross but you don't know where. The milky currents give up few secrets. Here the lake is open, but just a hundred yards out it is crusted with blue ice. You think if you manage to bomb a cast right to the edge you'll have some luck, but as hard as you try you can't even cast half the distance.

Birds congregate here like it's a festival. Out on the water, mallards and widgeons are cozied up together in rafts, and above them, careening like swallows, are the silvery vectors of gulls. From the land, sparrows flit between the bushes scanning for seeds and insects, and ptarmigan squabble from unseen coverts. Somehow existing within the trinity of land, air, and water, a single Arctic tern hovers over the exact place where the current meets the stagnation of the lake. His nose (here you can't be sure of the gender, but you go with it anyway) is sharp as a fighter jet, and it is pointed downward as a pair of keen little eyes survey the water. His wings beat frantically but his body is steadfast. He dives with perfect streamlined form, levitates over the water for a heartbeat, and plunges. You can't see if he's caught anything, but you assume he has. You get the sense that he doesn't waste many motions.

Inspired by his actions, you unwind the new fly line you've just bought, attach a sink-tip to the end, then a leader of fluorocarbon, and you tie on a smolt pattern. You like the way it looks in the water, how the bucktail gives it the slim profile of a salmon fry, how the composite-loop head sparkles like tiny green scales. Mostly you like it because you've designed it.

Your only qualm about today is that there is only *one* tern. If this were the heat of the smolt migration, and the mackinaw of lore were to be caught, you expect there'd be dozens of terns hovering above the silt. They'd lead you to that transition of current and still, of water and land, of a slack line and a tight one. You'd watch them dip, dive, swoop, hurtle and otherwise gloat about their capacity for flight.

One tern isn't bad news, though. He stays in the area as you feel your way along the lakebed. Your steps are hesitant because the lake drops off from wading depths to over twenty feet, and that's not a plunge you want to take today.

Cars rush along the highway, as far off as shooting stars, and you feel sorry for them. They don't know about the world beyond the asphalt. They don't know the muskrat that surfaces like a miniature submarine just to get a look at you, or the flotsam that laps against the sand, or the feel of fly line as it shoots through your hand and snaps against the reel in the final throw. They don't know the pleasing buzz of wasted time.

But you do. Somehow, you do. You haven't done anything special, really—you've simply followed the trail, slogged through a bit of dead mud, and stood out here in the rain long enough for the birds to see you as a fence post instead of a bipedal. It's something anybody could've done.

You start thinking about the tern again. He's come from Antarctica, a place as distant and dizzyingly vague as "the Moon." He's spent the Southern Hemisphere's summer on pack ice down there, dipping for pelagic minnows the same way he's dipping for young sockeyes right now. The fact that he's here, and you're look- ing at him, has the same odds-defying comfort as knowing the name of a star, and locating it within a never-ending sky full of billions of others. With luck, you think, he'll be joined soon by his company, and this place will become a cacophony of bird sounds and fish. The female terns will drop eggs and about the same time the salmon are streaking upriver to spawn and die this fall, the brood will be big enough to cross the globe. In the coddled time- lines of humans, such a concept is boggling.

After a few dozen casts that begin to feel programmed, you think about leaving. Normally you'd be overthinking the sink-rate of your line and the color of your fly and the speed of retrieve and all that rot, but not today. You're thinking about the tern and what he does (all the above life-history you learn later), and that gives you many unanswered things to toil over in the moment. You're fishing in the rain, doing it just for the hell of it, and thinking about absolutely nothing that has to do with your own world.

"Thanks," you might mutter as you leave, but the tern has disap- peared into the silver.

You want to tell him that you'll be back and to let you know when the smolt really start moving, but then you start to feel puny in the mind of a bird who's travelled the world.

Halfway back to the truck the rain stops. The air tastes as good as strong coffee on a frosty morning, or a cold malt beer after a day spent digging ditches, pounding fence posts, or any other farm sundry you grew up doing. Your legs and toes are cold, and you know the heater will feel all the better because of it. You'll drive those last two hundred miles in silence.

Knee-deep snow on the trail. A swamp spills over where the beavers have dammed it. The fox tracks follow in the opposite direction now, through the willows, heading north, and you stop to pee right where you imagine he did.

# FOUR: SOMETHING TO DO

I T'S SUCH A BRIGHT DAY THAT I MUST SQUINT just looking down at the gravel. There's a light wind rustling the trees, and even though the lake—more of a swamp, I suppose—is the highest it's been in recent memory, everything feels chapped. I pass a shirtless dude on a bike and it's only after I ask, "How's it goin'?" that I realize he's got a fly rod strapped to the back.

"S'alright," he says. His skin is leathery and thick and if this was anywhere else, he'd make a convincing surfer. "They're around, that's for sure."

I can only assume he means the pike because I've got a fly rod in my hand, too—but I suppose he could have meant anything. It doesn't really matter because next second, he's gone in a thin plume of dust, and I follow his tire tracks to try and spot the places he stopped.

The shooting range orchestra to the east plays one of its more famous pieces. Closer by, mallards yelp and dragonflies chatter on chitinous wings.

My steps are heavy down the dirt road because I'm wearing hip boots, and I suppose lugging them this far means I should use them. I hadn't really planned on fishing, to tell you the truth. The pike spawn is over, and I figured this place would be dried up, dotted with formerly submerged tennis balls and shotgun shells and all the other interesting things you could find in a drained bathtub. But I have to say, walking down the road with a six-weight and a bucktail fly in my hand, the place looks *fishy*. I'm not sure exactly what that means, but for me it meant the weeds were growing, the water was clear and enticing, and I could imagine a big ol' gator pike sunning himself and just waiting to slaughter something.

The track record for this place wasn't good, but it was the only place within a sane driving distance that wasn't flooded by runoff or riddled with triploid rainbows. Here's how it was: I was in Fairbanks packing up our apartment and trying to find a new renter so that Emmie and I could abandon our lease two months early. I was taking a break and I'd just finished perusing a used bookstore and was wondering what to do with the rest of my afternoon.

I thought of the lake (swamp) and figured why not. It was right down the road, it was a beautiful day, I could do with a little head-clearing, yadda yadda yadda. The whole affair was like a magazine at the dentist; not really your first choice but something to do, anyway. Did I mention it has a poor track record? In the six years I'd fished it—jeez, is that how long it's been?—I'd caught exactly two pike, and both laid end to end weren't much longer than my forearm. One time I took a raft out and fished Rapalas up and down every bank until I couldn't stand it anymore. The only strike I had was from a foot-long rainbow that threw a treble hook.

So, there I was, some number of years later, following the shirtless guy's bike tracks even though I knew perfectly well where I was going. I ducked down beneath the wall of alders and unhooked the fly from the keeper and started casting. Just like that.

I didn't see any pike, but that six-weight felt good after a long and record-cold winter. The absence of fish and the rhythmic swish-swash of casting coaxed my brain into a sort of daze, and I began considering all things past and present, homing in on some of them and discarding others without thought, like what yesterday's 10 o'clock meeting was about. I thought about renting a U-Haul to relay all of our possessions, which, once you start moving them, take up far more space than you remember. I thought about lazy afternoons I'd known before, the better of them spent just like this, fishing for no reason at all. I thought about my brother, Hank, and his impending choice: he was going to ask Taryn, his long-time girlfriend, to marry him soon. Stuff like that.

My mother, back home in Wyoming, had called me the day before and I could tell from the first word that something was wrong. I knew what it was before she said it, too. A few weeks earlier she'd found two baby raccoons—orphaned brothers—cuddled up in her strawberry patch and had been more-or-less nursing them back to health. At one point she thought one of them had died, but it was just so weak from being left without its mother and any discernible foraging skills that it was nearly comatose. She fed them routinely but kept them away from the house, and though I was 3,000 miles away, I felt like I was part of it. She'd send pictures and videos of those little buggers climbing face-first down an elm tree, or wrestling each other off a stump to be the first to get fed. I think all along I knew better than to get too attached to them, but just like with any pet, I suppose, that's hard to do. You know one day too soon they'll go and break your heart. I was even dumb enough to convince Mom to name them.

Long story short, one of them had fallen fifty feet out of the elm tree and crushed his skull.

It's just like I told Mom, though: stuff like that happens every day, every minute in nature, we're just never connected to any of it to notice. I was casting fifty feet into an open spot in the weeds about the size of a hula hoop, trying hard not to think about that little raccoon I'd never met. You know how that goes. There was a spectacular absence of answers, and I was trying to find all of them.

I didn't catch anything that afternoon, and I drove home in a truck about as comfortable as the inside of a microwave oven. I should just write that stupid lake off as no good. It's never been anything but a pit of wasted time and sunburns and pond scum. I get home and read one of the books I bought and make a frozen pizza and eat it on our couch that's quite literally returning to dust before my eyes. The apartment feels like a bachelor pad, and I just know that words would echo through the emptiness if I would say some. We'll be leaving this city in two months' time, and chances are good that we'll never return for more than a vacation. When that happens, there are a million other places I'll fish before I go back to the swamp, so—more likely than not—that was the last time I ever fished it.

# FIVE: RED SHIRT

I T'S FUNNY HOW WHEN YOU PLAN SOMETHING and start looking forward to it—anything from a quick weekend getaway to a
full-blown vacation—it's a little difficult to believe when it finally
arrives. Not that it isn't probable, of course; it's all part of the plan
that you yourself designed. It's just that you spend all that time
imagining how things will go, worrying about flight itineraries or
if the canoe rental will spring a leak, and then, somehow, all your
illusions spin to a confluence and the trip happens. Most of the
time, things don't pan out exactly as you plan, but that's just as well.
If everything happened the way you imagined it would, the act of
going would be redundant, wouldn't it?

For me, the moment when I knew we were there, and that this
was no longer something to look forward to but rather something
to be *in*, came while sitting in a green canoe with Emmie at the
helm and a thousand acres of northern pike water ahead. We were
making our annual pilgrimage to Red Shirt Lake.

I first explored this place three years earlier, and those initial
trips suggested that it was a place worth revisiting if not all for the

fishing than for the wilderness experience that comes from being nestled three miles off any drivable surface. Not only could a person expect to hook fifty pike on a good day and see more loons and bald eagles in an hour than some others may see in a lifetime, but the lake was equipped with six public-use cabins that could be rented on a shoestring-and-ramen budget. That was great for me at the time because, although I was employed, it was seasonal work, and my finances were about to be drained by something made of precious metal.

Those first few trips were good for getting a lay of the lake. Even though I spent many a day of childhood trolling for walleyes with my Uncle "Booge" (my brother Hank's infantile derangement of "Uncle Bill"), I still find lakes and reservoirs as indecipherable as modern calculus. Eventually I surmounted this, at least in the case of Red Shirt, and I combed the banks enough to come up with the ages-old formula: weeds equal pike. On subsequent trips it made me look like I knew at least part of what I was doing, first for a visiting friend from Wyoming and then for Emmie, who was my longtime girlfriend at the time. Both agreed that the fishing was "pretty good," which allowed me a few sighs of relief. Bringing someone to your spot is like showing someone your art—*you* think it's good, but someone else could just as easily think it's a pile of rat crap.

Incidentally, on July 31st of that first exploration year I proposed to Emmie out front of one of those public-use cabins, and for reasons I'll never know she said yes. I don't really remember the fishing that weekend.

So, THERE WE WERE AGAIN, BACK FOR A FISHING TRIP disguised as an early two-year anniversary celebration. Just Emmie and I, a pair of excessively heavy backpacks, and a canoe that looked like it could've been used as a battering ram at the Battle of Lepanto. Part of the reason I was in such disbelief to be there was that the previous year's planned trip had been barred by a wildfire of biblical proportions. It was proof that you could spend all the time you wanted planning something, but Mother Nature has the final say. We passed much of the fire's aftermath on the hike in.

It was three miles leading from a campground at the end of the Nancy Lake Parkway to the lake which is only accessed by foot or float plane. It's on level ground and weaves through mosquito-ridden woods. I would make the obligatory joke about Alaskan mosquitoes being big enough to haul you off your feet, or that Alaska's state bird is not the willow ptarmigan but in fact the mosquito itself, but I won't. Even the most far-fetched wives' tales have some roots, and whether we believe them or not, there are some chilling fossils from Permian-era mosquitoes that were the size of ospreys.

Other than that, the hike was pleasant. Normally you can run into a spruce grouse hen and her brood doddering like drunks down the trail, but they must've been elsewhere. An assortment of passerines pinged from high in the canopy, and we found the wild raspberry patch that would have been delicious were it in fruit. Once at the lake we found some poor sap's abandoned bear spray (a high dollar find in these parts) and launched the canoe.

Being that we couldn't check in to the cabin until noon and only had to paddle about a half mile to get there, it made sense to fish a little bit on the way. The day was resounding blue, clouds fat as Spanish warships marched overhead, and the lake stretched beyond sight like a floor of chrome, rippling gently in sync with the sudden acceleration of a Cessna engine. Soon we started passing loons, many of which would let us get within photo range before diving without a sound. Then they would surface and cry with the volume of blaring trumpets, the echoes wedging themselves somewhere in our souls. According to ornithologists, these cries are merely the loon's way of playing Marco Polo, but I can't help but think it sounds a lot nicer than screaming "Over here!" at the top of your lungs.

Just across the bay from the boat launch was the weed patch where Emmie caught her first pike almost three years ago. I remember it well because I had a ring buried in the tackle box (the last place she'd ever look). Then there was the place I caught a pike on a bottlecap per a bet with my friend Orrin. There was the drop-off where I hooked what had to be a 30-plus-incher—you know how those stories go—but lost it boatside; there was the white shack marking one of the best spots on the lake for topwater fishing; and, looming largest in my memory, the exact patch of gravel on the beach of Noah's Island where I got down on one knee. Red Shirt was an old friend we hadn't seen in a while.

NORTHERN PIKE HAVE ALWAYS BEEN A BIT MYSTICAL TO ME. They weren't found within a hundred miles of the farm where I grew up in southeast Wyoming, and even though that's a trivial distance to drive for fish, we had stuff that was much better to eat (walleye, catfish, trout) just down the road. As with most things out of a kid's reach, I became obsessed with pike. I don't know if it was their size, the galactic arrangement of golden spots lining their flanks, or their strange anatomy that put them somewhere between a snake and a crocodile; all I knew is that I wanted to catch one. There were tiger muskies in a reservoir about a half hour away, but rumors suggested that they'd been fished out in the 1990s and the few reconnaissance trips Dad took Hank and I on proved fruitless. And anyway, tiger muskies aren't *pike*. The one lake in Wyoming with a reliable pike population is Keyhole Reservoir up in the Devil's Tower country, and one summer when I was ten years old the stars aligned. Hank had a baseball tournament just around the corner in Gillete and Dad brought the bass boat up.

We didn't catch the fabled pike of Keyhole (though we did catch a mess of black crappie and smallmouth bass beneath some Wild West limestone cliffs), and it wouldn't be until I was 21 years old that I caught my first pike in a dumpy and previously mentioned little swamp in Fairbanks. My childhood perception of the fish must have left a mark somewhere, though, because entering pike territory still ushers an unspoken reverence like that of stepping into rattlesnake or bear country.

Emmie and I swung down the lake casting frogs to openings in mats of weeds and algal blooms, bringing a few in and losing a few others. It wasn't anything to write home about yet, but the thing about Red Shirt is that it coughs up 40-plus-inchers on occasion, and a behemoth just shy of the state record at 38 pounds was caught here within my lifetime.

By that point it was time to unload our ballast of superfluous crap and have lunch, so we pulled up to cabin number 4. The outside looked like a cabin you might find at a retreat bible camp, and the inside looked like a cabin that you might find at a retreat bible camp for delinquents. It was a roof over our heads and a platform for a sleeping pad, which was fine because that's what it was advertised under and, like I said, it was dirt cheap. Anyway, we'd hauled the real camp luxuries in on our backs: squashy sleeping bags, a two-person hammock, a JetBoil and fuel, and the item voted "Most Catastrophic to Forget," the coffee percolator and a bag of fresh grounds. We dumped it all gratefully in the corner.

Somebody had filleted pike on the picnic table outside, so we ate our lunch within a galaxy of peevish black flies. I think this may have worked to my advantage, however, because Emmie got so fed up with them that she demanded we get in the canoe at once to escape them. Fine by me.

We cruised the shoreline all afternoon looking for pike, seeing very few fish but instead many shadows of fish. To tell pike apart from logs you just scan for their pectoral fins. Then you'd see the fish—the predator—lying in wait, their protruding lower jaws making them look like a kid on the brink of an unholy tantrum. You'd make a cast within a few feet of their head and they'd turn for it upon entry. A few strips and they'd align themselves like rifle sights, noodling along behind the fly and just daring it to flee. The moment when they accelerate forward and flash upon the fly like the glint of a blade must be one of the most electric events in all of fly-fishing. You're somehow *within* the most predatory of spectacles, and the fact that it took a fishing rod to make it happen gives it the pleasing air of exclusivity.

Dinner that evening was a simple affair with canned chicken and some curry mix things heated up in a fry pan. As I prodded stuff with the spatula, I felt like I was still swaying in the canoe, more proof than the stinging burn on my neck that we'd spent enough time fishing.

As we ate, I perused the cabin journal. This had been written in by dozens if not hundreds of state parks patrons over the years. It gave the place a tincture of camaraderie that transcended time and space; even though I'd never met or was likely to meet any of these people, I could see all of us sitting around a campfire and talking about our time at Cabin 4. Here a couple of fishermen named Daniel and Matt had spent two days in September of 2016 fishing obsessively for pike and marking the lengths of their catches (their biggest was a respectable 34-incher). Others had spent anniversary trips here. There was the occasional bit of good advice (lighting mosquito coils above the window before bed), and some bad advice ('the picnic table makes a great filleting station!'), along with several assurances that there was either a squirrel or a derelict gentleman living in the roof. A few records were written in a utilitarian's shorthand (March 23, 2018: 'Ice way too thin'), leaving the unsaid up to imagination. More entries than not praised the immaculate quality of the outhouse. In any case, the journal made for entertaining reading, but once was enough. Eventually I watched the smoke from the mosquito coil drift like cobwebs long enough to fall asleep.

We awoke to the workday chatter of birds. I was up first, and the heat of the night before had settled to the slimy chill of Alaskan morning.

The first order of business in any camp worth its salt is to make the coffee. Soon water was rumbling in the percolator. The spout belched steam. I started getting a little contemplative, thinking about how some people are so far removed from nature that they don't even know where their coffee comes from. You ask me, standing there looking out at rank upon rank of mosquitos on the window screen and the sleepy painting of Red Shirt Lake stirring itself to life, I think more cups of coffee should have the grounds in them, just like more steaks should have some fat on them and salmon fillets should include the skin. But that's just a six a.m. thought. Take it or leave it.

Camp coffee is usually best as a sludge but mind you don't over brew it and get that metallic aftertaste. That doesn't help anybody. I managed to get ours somewhere between high-proof espresso and motor oil, and it tasted okay, but I made a mental note to bring some more expensive stuff next time. My next order of business was to scramble some eggs and boil some water to replenish our depleted supply. Emmie packed up and we started a fire in the woodstove and otherwise bummed around for an hour or two. The weed flats of pike were still warming up.

I like those kinds of trips. No rush. No goal other than wasting time. You can see the outlines of a plan, but as they'd appear on paper they're 'tentative'—which means you can paddle over to the other side of the lake to check out the creek for no other reason than being curious, and you can forage haphazardly for black morels, and you can sit and stare at damsel nymphs wiggling in the sand because, you believe, you've got all the time in the world. Though I'm a run-of-the-mill planner myself and have been known to exhibit bouts of anxiety from lack of structure, sometimes it's nice—necessary—to throw it all out the window. You forget about the rat race of traffic on the paved roads and start to see things as loops; as whimsical ebbs and flows of nature where the sculpin eats the damsel nymph, and the pike eats the sculpin, and the eagle spears the pike and airdrops its skeleton into a quiet backwater where it might become fossilized but probably gets forgotten. Things that once felt significant like deadlines and projects suddenly become as trivial as a children's show. You start to condemn whoever it was that said work must take place from nine to five and that getaways to places like this were to be earned disproportionately from the summation of timesheets.

Soon we were fishing our way down the southern side of a large island, where a nice mud and weed flat stretched as far as I could see. And hovering in between the weeds, like bullets loaded into a chamber, waiting, were the shadows of pike. I settled into a rhythm of stalking these fish, focusing myself into a trance that was interrupted only by the sounds of breaking water.

If you've ever seen a moose cross the highway, you know there isn't a more awkward and gangling creature on the planet. But boy can they swim. Emmie and I turned the canoe to see not one, but *three* of them making passage from the mainland to the island (a half mile or so). It was a mom and a pair of twins, the smaller of which kept piggybacking the other. Before I could say "pike," they vanished into the spruce.

By then it was about lunch, and we paddled to our second cabin of the trip (Cabin 3), where I'd previously gone from bachelor to engaged in one swoop of the knee. It felt like a homecoming if not a visitation to hallowed ground. The wooden bench from our previous stay was gone and I could only assume that someone had gotten desperate somewhere between then and now and fed the fire pit with it. Just like with the guy that wrote the ice was too thin, I could only offer retrospective support. Hopefully, they survived.

IT'S SINCE BEEN MADE CLEAR TO ME THAT MOSQUITOES are like gases; that is, they fill whatever volume they're contained within. Even if it's only one. *Especially* if it's only one. As Emmie and I wound ourselves down to try and get some sleep that night, our ears knew only the peevishness of the insect, first in the far corner like a memory, then circling our heads like an electron around a nucleus. I caught a glimpse of him in my peripheral vision and struck, clapping my hands. The buzzing stopped. His corpse lay flattened against my palm. But then, another . . . another.

Emmie managed to drift off by then, but I was stuck listening to a dentist's drill. It wasn't that big of a deal because I had a book to finish and a new one to start, but still.

By midnight things hadn't improved. I killed a few more mosquitoes only to discover they were replaced by two more. I checked over the windows and door and found no evidence of their point of entry. They were just *appearing* out of thin air.

As much as I wanted to be asleep, it was a nice time to be awake. The sky was aglow in the midnight sun, a combination of deep-space blue and rusty orange, and boreal owls were fluting from anonymous perches. I started thinking about things as I tend to do when the world around me is either idle or I make it that way.

Marriage and fishing are quite alike. People who don't understand one or the other either find it pointless, cruel, an obligation, or some varying combination of these; while the people that *do* understand know it to be one of the greatest gifts and duties that God ever gave to our species. That's not to say that either are perfect, because in the whole of my existence no two things have given me greater fits of frustration, it's just that they're both among the few elements of life that have turned out to be worth the trouble.

A good wife is as indispensable as your favorite fly rod; as rare and stunning as the best fish of your life and as steadfast as camp coffee. She's kind and understanding and thoughtful, and even if she doesn't have the fishing bug altogether herself, she accepts that you do and keeps you from becoming homeless on a riverbank

somewhere. As I stand there in my skivvies with the drone of mosquitoes trembling in my ears, I realize that Emmie is all of that and
more. She's dawn on a September trout stream, dusk on a pike lake
as still as glass in midsummer, on a night just like this. She's everything I love for all the reasons I can't put words to.

NEXT MORNING I'VE GOT A SPLITTING HEADACHE from all the
water I didn't drink, so I make up for it by brewing some coffee.
When you're fishing for days on end, I like to think that God for-
gives the abuses you put your body through. Part of you wants
to be hydrated, cleaned, and polished again, but some other part
wants to stay out where you have the freedom to starve and ache
like a dog with arthritis.

It's about then that I start wondering where the last two days
went. It's like I've woken up from an unplanned nap. The reality, of
course, is that time goes neither faster nor slower when you're on
a trip like this. It remains as it's been since the dawn of time; since
the giant mosquitoes buzzed the Earth. I think, rather, that it's our
sudden abandoning of all the things that normally *keep track* of
the time, the guiding shackles of humankind, that becomes so per-
plexing. We just don't know what to do with ourselves.

Emmie and I have a nice breakfast and sit out on the hammock before we pack things away. We have no regards for time
other than our checkout at noon. We walk slowly around the
island and imagine being stranded here. It's not that disturbing
of a thought.

It feels premature to be going back, and we both dread the
asphalt and pixels of our other world. Soon we'll be swallowed by
a gilded hellscape where alcoholism, obesity, and a deafening lack
of courtesy reign supreme, where cars travel like mice in a maze.
We'll take a bet that someday, mankind will end up eating each
other just like pike do.

But before any of that, while we're still out here all innocent and sunburnt, I remind myself that we did what we came to do. We caught some pike, tasted some clean air, and fittingly celebrated a milestone of commitment. When you finish a good day of work, you celebrate, even if it's silent and takes place only in your own head. Our celebration, as we loaded the canoe and set out to have just a few more casts before heading home, came with the cry of a loon. He was far away, and we couldn't see him, but we didn't need to.

Back at the parking lot, hours later, I meet a boy who's been ravaged by the mosquitoes to the point that he looks like he's got chicken pox. He tells me he caught his first pike, and I can't help but think myself at the same age would've been jealous.

# SIX: DRIVING THOUGHTS

M OST OF THE TIME, I'D RATHER EAT CYANIDE than drive in a city. But out there in the big empty, where the streets turn to highways and get long and unbroken, driving is one of my favorite things to do. You can turn on some music, sip at some coffee, and drive with your knee if you want to (and are skilled at it, otherwise you'll find a cozy spot in a ditch somewhere). In Alaska, these long solitary stretches of road are among the prettiest in the world, and often I must remind myself to look at where the road is going and not the magnesium glow of far-off mountains.

Driving to fishing spots is the best kind of driving there is, short of road-trip driving where your next destination isn't really known. If you're headed to a place you've fished before, you start wondering if it will be as good (or as bad) as the last time you were there. You think back on all the great trout or grayling or salmon you've hooked, you recall that time you almost ran fly rod-first into a black bear on a gravel bar. If it's a place you haven't been before, you can't help but imagine what it will be like. The potential of untrod water is as exquisite as anything in the world.

When I'm headed for a stream, whether I've been there before or not, I aim to be fishing by the time the sun is rising. In summertime Alaska, that means I usually leave around two or three a.m. Being on the road that early always makes me feel a little selfish; no one else is out, I can drive as fast or as slow as I please, and the faint rind of the moon seems especially bright just for me. I might even see a lynx if I'm lucky.

Today, though, I'm not going fishing (at least not planning on it), so the departure time is something a little more human: nine o'clock. I'm headed back up to Fairbanks for what I hope to the Dear Lord is our last moving-out-of-the-apartment crusade. It'll be exciting—a little melancholy—when we shut that door for the final time, but there's a lot of work to do before then. I stop for gas in Glennallen and then I'm tethered to the road for four hours.

It's a common joke that in Alaska there are only two seasons: winter and road construction. This proves to be true as I head north on the Richardson Highway, which, between Glennallen and Paxson, is a combination of frost heaves, potholes as deep as a five-gallon bucket, and strips of raw gravel. The drivers in front of me slow down to thirty for the gravel, which makes me chuckle. Evidently, they didn't spend their teenage years doing seventy on the county road just to make it to school on time. That's another thing about driving—I hate the stigma that because I'm young and male, I drive fast. The fact that it's pure truth is beside the point. As my dad will vehemently tell you, fast doesn't necessarily mean unsafe, and the way I look at it, I'm far more aware of things when I drive fast for the simple fact that I must be. You ante up when the stakes are high.

Anyway, I was stopped twice for construction projects. We had to wait for some guy to sweep dirt off the asphalt.

Sometimes I like waving to people and sometimes I don't. Where I grew up in Wyoming, waving was a requirement; if you didn't, people assumed you were either an asshole or, worse, an out-of-stater. Even on the highway people always waved. Today's a day I feel like waving for no good reason at all, but I only get three returned waves out of fifty vehicles I pass. I know that because I kept track on a sticky note, and you ask me, that's a bad record. I believe it's got something to do with the speed limit (i.e., higher wave-rates correspond with lower speed limits), but still. When Emmie and I end up settling down somewhere for good, I'm going to use whether people wave or not as a deciding factor.

That's just an example of the kind of crap I think about while I'm driving. Most of the time I worry about things like finishing up the restoration on a 1957 canned-ham camper that Emmie and I bought a few years ago, or starting my teaching internship in August, or if the Gulkana will ever slow down and clear up so I can have a shot at the king salmon. I plan fishing trips that may or may not happen. I think about the world we're living in.

Boy, you know it's a long drive when you start thinking about politics. If you ask me, political discourse doesn't belong within a hundred yards of any fish-bearing body of water. 2020 has been a tumultuous year, though, and I would be remiss if I didn't at least provide a context for the seasons in which all this unbridled fishing has taken place.

It was February that people started worrying a little about the novel coronavirus, and it was March that things like toilet paper shortages, "social distancing", and shelter-in-place mandates became popular and, as they say, a certain arrangement of organic molecules started hitting the fan. The great partisan divide that tends to bisect any issue (political or not) started grouping people into "Mask Wearers" and "Non-Mask Wearers." In one corner you have the people that give you funny looks when you walk into Sportsman's Warehouse wearing a bandana, and on the other you have people who look mortally offended if your nose is exposed in a parking lot.

Many others have much more to say about the events of 2020. I will say only that humans have evolved significantly in every sector besides good sense and how to treat one another—which is why, I suppose, when that certain element starts hitting the fan and pandemics and police killings and riots start popping up like ditch fires gone awry, the government deems it prudent to treat us like livestock.

All right, ladies and gents. End of soapbox. There's a good grayling stop ahead.

❦

YOU DON'T WANT TO HEAR ABOUT PACKING UP the apartment any more than I liked completing it, so let's just say I'm headed out of Fairbanks three days later, unable to see out the rearview because my truck is crammed with strangely shaped items like porcelain lamps and bar stools and bathroom vanities. There's a potted plant in the passenger seat, a seedling black spruce that I transplanted from the driveway last summer. It somehow endured the winter in an old tire and is growing new buds like little caterpillars. I've tended it carefully because I like the weight of time that trees can hold. I like the idea that I can look back on it someday and remember our first apartment. I don't go so far as to fasten the seat belt around it, though.

It's six in the evening when I leave, which means if I drive normally, I'll roll onto my in-laws' farmyard between ten-thirty and eleven o'clock. Bit of a late bedtime for me, but hey—it's summer in Alaska so the sun stays out forever.

Considering this and reminding myself that I will be homebound all winter and will kick myself for squandering an opportunity, I stop and have a try at the lake trout, or mackinaw (again). I'm somewhere between hopeful and hopeless, watching the lake stretch away as far as I can see, knowing my casts will paint over a mere spec of the place. Then again, the sun is setting, and perhaps my luck will change. I cast, wade, and test the soft lakebed all the way out to the limits of my hip boots. I reason that I ought to try somewhere else. I don't think Einstein was referring to fishing when he said doing something over and over the same way while expecting a different result was the definition of madness, but I figure it can't hurt my chances.

The trail forks near a lone spruce, and I follow it past a grave-yard of old oil and soup cans. More likely than not it was an ancient trash burning pit for whoever owned the cabin farther down the trail. Ice fishermen from the winter have discarded their own arti-facts here; Budweiser cans and a punctured gasoline jug. A willow ptarmigan is cackling from somewhere as I step over a crushed shotgun shell.

The lake is as smooth as foil and the sun makes it look glow-ing hot. Around me the silence of solitude thunders, so much that I feel like I've been swallowed. I'm far enough from the road that the cars, trucks, and RVs driving on it look like traveling pixels, and I know that it takes several seconds for the white noise of their engines to reach me.

Rises pock the surface here and there. I watch carefully because they're so subtle; was it a mosquito grazing the surface film, or the gentle lips of a grayling? A cast near one of these tells the tale. The fly is sucked under in an ephemeral whorl, then I'm connected to something lean but good-sized. The glare off the lake keeps me from seeing exactly what it is.

I'm giddy as a schoolboy, giddy as I would've been when I was five years old, and Dad took my hands in his and clasped them around a fishing pole. Just as I draw the fish in to cradle it, the tippet swinging toward me like a pendulum, the fish gives a quick rush lakeward and throws the hook. The next cast I snap the fly off in the bushes. Such is fishing.

Looking out into that big open country beyond the lake, I real-ize that Alaska is a place where you can drive forever if you want to. But if you look on the map at the area covered by roads, it's bogglingly insignificant. The rest of the state is there—millions upon millions of acres of it—but somehow not. The roadless area has seasons that are defined by things other than road construction; the birth of moose calves or the blooming of fireweed or the return of king salmon.

I fish for too long. Long enough for the sun to start setting, anyway, which occurs at around midnight. The sky gets twilight-gray, and the clouds dissipate and the world seems to settle down. I chase the rises of grayling up and down the bank and try to lead the fish, failing far more often than I succeed. I bring a few lovely fish to hand. They're so cold my fingers tingle as I let them go. A beaver makes his patrol along the shoreline.

I don't think about much as I drive home through the wee hours. It feels like the brink of a wonderful summer full of late nights and early mornings and being tired all the time but being okay with that. I pass so few cars that I'm the one that forgets to wave.

It's one a.m. by the time I near the farm, and as I cross the Klutina River I wonder if the sockeyes are finally running there. The campgrounds are sure packed enough to suggest it. And while I'd rather eat cyanide than fish alongside the hordes of weekenders, if I get up early enough, I can beat them to it and have some fun.

# SEVEN: SLAVE TO THE SOCKEYE

Y OU CAN ALWAYS TELL WHEN SALMON SEASON is finally here in the Copper River Valley of Alaska. And I don't mean by the Fish and Game Department's sonar counts, or by the motorcades of campers and truck-trailers that start constipating the highways. I'm talkin' about my fly tying vise and the area surrounding it, which, in early June, starts to lose some of the drab charm that comes with tying dozens of dry flies and small nymphs and instead takes on the gaudy electric glow of a strip club. Marabou dyed in shades found nowhere in nature drifts listlessly through the air.

Pacific salmon are unique in that they stop feeding once they leave saltwater to spawn in freshwater. This, of course, doesn't mean you can't catch them—it just becomes a matter of aggravating over enticing. Hence the neon abominations littering my tying bench. Sockeyes, however, are the exception. Even in the ocean, they feed exclusively on zooplankton and shrimp, giving them somewhat of an immunity to the tactics employed for their brethren. The only reliable way to catch them becomes snagging them in the mouth, which is done by drifting a heavily weighted rig on the bottom and trying to 'floss' a hook into the salmon's maw. On some streams you can see the fish and target specific individuals, but on a glacial river like the Klutina (where I choose to fish and where the water is opaque as a protein shake), you're basically playing darts in the dark. This can be both a lot of fun and frustrating as hell; you never know when you're going to hook one, but you can also spend days on end drifting hooks past nothing and not know it. The whole thing shouldn't work, but somehow, sometimes, it does.

Compounding upon this difficulty of capture, sockeyes in the Copper River drainage can be horrendously temperamental. Last year the run peaked around the 15th of June and just over a million fish entered the river system by August. The year before the run was around 700,000 strong and the peak came in the first few weeks of July. Typically, I start thinking about sockeyes around the 5th of June, then by the 15th I'm driving slow past the river to see if anyone's fishing yet. This year, I'd heard reports of hit-and-miss fishing as early as the 10th. The final moving trip to Fairbanks kept me tied down until Sunday the 20th, and by then the campgrounds were as busy as the Daytona 500. I *could* have gone that Saturday afternoon, but the public access water south of the bridge was swarming with people. Not my thing.

Being that Emmie's parents lived so close, and therefore now that I did, I had the resident luxury of coming back whenever I wanted to. With the rods in the truck, I set the alarm for the next morning at an hour when only owls should be awake.

IT'S FOUR O'CLOCK OR SO WHEN I ROLL OUT OF THE DRIVEWAY. Solitary fishing aside, the real benefit of getting up that early is that I can make the coffee before my father-in-law. It's not that his coffee is notoriously bad, it's just that it's better classified as tea. I require something more of the "warp a spoon" variety.

Outside, the world is sleepy. The sky is the same color as a fresh sockeye's back and there's only one other car at the bridge. It's a boxy, matter-of-fact vehicle in turquoise, the make a Suzuki, the model a Samurai. There are dipnets and fly rods lashed to a roof rack, both hallmarks of a well-rounded adventurer. I can deal with that. Anyone who beats me to the river has my respect.

It's been a while since I've fished here. Being that the run is so volatile, it's a lot harder to drag yourself toward a mere hope and a wish than it is to chase grayling, trout, and salmon you can see in other places. And anyway, we lived five hours away until this summer. Now that I'm just down the road, I feel a sense of obligation to give it a try.

The path is quiet, well-trod like a goat trail. It's only a couple of minutes to our spot, though most anglers go much further. It's a place Emmie and I staked out through much trial and error five years ago; a seam between slow and fast currents, and this year, there's a log jam that's created a pinch-point in the run. The river churns like an explosion, containing within it the crumbling of mountains and the crashing of glaciers as it barrels seaward. I drop the tackle box and gaze stupidly into its silvery-blue flow.

Despite how it may look or be described, there is an art to flossing the sockeye. I use sections of quarter-inch lead wire to get my flies within a foot or so of the bottom. Usually, you start out with too much of this weight, and you'd better snip it back otherwise you'll get snagged and lose the whole rig. You want to just tap the top of the riverbed, the sensation of which is like dragging your rod tip over a washboard. Most anglers don't even cast this weight-and-fly arrangement, they merely let out ten feet of line and toss it by hand in a maneuver that's been called 'the Kenai flip.' The idea is that fish run so close to the bank that you only need a short drift to hook them, and it makes for more drifts per hour if you don't have to mess with a bail. I suppose in that case a fly rod would make it easier, but I use a spinning setup because flinging that kind of load on a fly rod seems about as wrong as towing a stock trailer with a Lamborghini. The actual drift is like swinging wet flies. Any stops that you detect are either a rock, a snarl of entombed rigs from yesteryear, or a fish. My first strike is for a rock and, unable to retrieve it successfully, I stoop to tie another rig.

That's the other thing about the Klutina that makes it so hard to fish: the innards of this river have eaten a small fortune in hooks and lead.

Fifteen minutes and I decide to go check out the mouth. I've never been down that far, and I'm not really taking myself or the fishing too seriously this morning. The river's noise fades in and out as I weave through trees, and where a gentle backwater meets the river, I run into the owner of the Suzuki Samurai. He's an older gentleman in a leather vest (which I'm guessing he fashioned himself out of a moose he harvested), and he makes mechanic, patient casts.

He turns out to be a man of few (actually zero) words. He merely answers my inquisitions of "How's it goin'?" and "Any luck?" with a grunt and a single shake of his head.

There wasn't much to see at the mouth other than the gargantuan flow of the Klutina meeting the gargantuan (and somehow muddier) flow of the Copper. The water I'm looking at will spin and tumble through some of the most rugged country on Earth and end up on the coast of Japan someday. Maybe it'll turn to rain that will fall on me somewhere years from now.

I return to our spot mostly out of sentiment. It's really not about where you fish. It's having the stoic resolve to make drift after drift and tie rig after rig. Over and over. The hour grows later and the after-hours silence I once enjoyed is replaced by fishermen. They materialize behind me, alone or in groups, nodding at me, heading to better grounds, wondering what in the heck that kid's doing this close to the bridge. I began to wonder the same thing, so you can imagine my surprise when I set the hook into something very much alive.

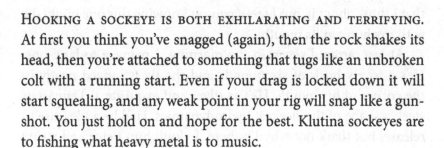

HOOKING A SOCKEYE IS BOTH EXHILARATING AND TERRIFYING. At first you think you've snagged (again), then the rock shakes its head, then you're attached to something that tugs like an unbroken colt with a running start. Even if your drag is locked down it will start squealing, and any weak point in your rig will snap like a gunshot. You just hold on and hope for the best. Klutina sockeyes are to fishing what heavy metal is to music.

The first one I hook stuns me. Plain and simple. I'm pretty sure my mouth hung open the entire fight. From his first leap, bursting from the water like the Saturn V bound for orbit, I could tell he was hooked fairly in the mouth (the requirement for a legally retained fish). The drag whines, the reel scratches like an old record as I winch him in. Just as I'm about to pull him onto the rocks, he flips and the ounce of lead on my rig slingshots back toward me. The hook's come free. I must sit down a moment and wait for the thundering of my blood to calm.

The second fish is equally bewildering. People will tell you how it feels and how you'll *know* it's a fish and not a rock when the rig stops, but that's a load of bull. We're all clueless. Everything feels like a rock, and you just set the hook in a bunch of erratic Hail Marys and occasionally you poke something edible. The sockeye gives me a few furious headshakes before the hook rips out. Insert expletive. Cast again if you can see straight.

The third salmon ran me so fast I couldn't adjust the drag and the 25-pound braid snapped like tying thread. I might have crumpled to my knees about then and lamented on the death of my angling ego. It had been so long since I'd tangled with these fish that I'd forgotten to respect them. These are salmon between four and ten pounds that have travelled hundreds of river miles already and still have a way to go. They're muscly, tenacious, and assisted by water that would kill me if I tried to swim in it. They're headed upriver to slowly wither, turn red, drop eggs and milt, and be eaten alive by fungus and rot. They give themselves, their entire lives, to one thing. I guess losing something like that isn't so bad, the more that I think about it, but I feel a pang at knowing this one might die with my hook in its mouth.

At last, around seven in the morning, I manage to land one. He's a lovely buck of six pounds and the fly is lodged neatly in the corner of his mouth. He's as silver and exquisite as Damascus steel; a shape of the sleekest hydrodynamics. He'd be a pleasure to release, but that's not why I'm here. I clonk him twice and string him through the gills with baling twine.

The morning bloats to afternoon, and I snag two fish which I release. The crowd grows, anglers line up on the opposite bank, and more shadows pass behind me headed downstream. Then, a single angler, heading back to the road. It's the old man in the moose vest, a fat sockeye dangling from one of his fingers. My heart glows for some reason at knowing he caught one, but I don't say anything, and neither does he.

I RETURN THE NEXT DAY.

The air is slimy and thick like fish mucus. The Samurai is back exactly where he was the day before. I think about what his name is—Elliott's the best I can come up with—before I decide to just call him the Samurai. I'm not fishing for a half hour before he passes me with his limit of three. He gives me a two-fingered wave on the way by.

I fish with the confidence that my luck will be the same, but four mundane hours later, I'm empty-handed. I hooked a fish for a split-second—long enough to see it breach like a dolphin—but that was the only event of note. A morning like that can make you wonder if the run is over, and if the dismally small sockeye numbers reported by the biologists are true. As I was packing up, another guy with red hair and a NASCAR cap came toddling down

into my spot and greeted me with a question:
"What the heck do you use around here?"

I looked around at my obvious lack of salmon and thought, *you're asking* me? But then I popped open the tackle box and showed him my little array of strip-club-colored flies. He scratched his head a little.

"You mean you don't use these?" His rod was equipped with a fat silver spoon lure.

I sent him on his way with a few of my hand-tied flies, along with some tips for rigging and honing his drift. I figured I'd never see him again and could only wonder if he'd put my advice to good use, but either way it felt good to think that I'd helped him. As much tooth enamel as I grind on account of seeing other fishermen on my turf, I find that most of them are real good people, and a few of them, even, I wouldn't mind sharing a beer with. It's just that most of the time I don't ever get to know any of them; we come and go through each other's lives like milepost markers on a highway.

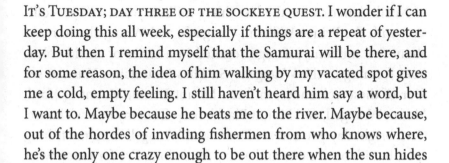

It's Tuesday; day three of the sockeye quest. I wonder if I can keep doing this all week, especially if things are a repeat of yesterday. But then I remind myself that the Samurai will be there, and for some reason, the idea of him walking by my vacated spot gives me a cold, empty feeling. I still haven't heard him say a word, but I want to. Maybe because he beats me to the river. Maybe because, out of the hordes of invading fishermen from who knows where, he's the only one crazy enough to be out there when the sun hides and you can still see your breath. I know nothing about him except that he's just like me.

The fishing becomes patterned—making the same sweeps over and over and over, occasionally snagging and moving up or downstream and yanking on the line hoping like hell it comes loose—and every now and then the pattern gets broken by defiant anadromous life. It's still early when I get the first fish. He's a big old buck of seven pounds; the kind that runs, leaps, and shoots some pure adrenaline into your system. His gill plates shimmer emerald-blue, his body goes from gunmetal on the back to pure silver on his belly. Looking down at him, I can't help but feel lucky. The Wrangell Mountains are shrouded in rainclouds and the drizzly weather of the weekend is still holding on. But there aren't many feelings better than catching a sockeye.

I don't catch anything the rest of the morning. I just stand there waving graphite and occasionally I slog back to the bank for a fresh gulp of coffee or to tie new rigs when I lose them. The in-between is filled with fleetingly dumb observations that I can't remember, a few Taylor Swift songs, and a couple of thoughts about rocks.

The Klutina runs through an area steeped in tumultuous geological history. Like most of Alaska, the area is made up of 'exotic' terranes—that is, chunks of land that came from elsewhere. The Wrangellia and Chugach terranes make up the bulk of the Copper River Valley, and both are subdivided by the Border Range Fault on one end and the Denali Fault on the other. Further to the south, the Yakutat terrane has been gliding along the west coast of North America for the last thirty million years, and its collision with the Prince William, Chugach, and Wrangellia terranes about five million years ago resulted in a series of shield volcanoes forming in the Wrangell - St. Elias Mountains. You can see four of these volcanoes, in fact—Mount Drum, Mount Sanford, Mount Wrangell, and Mount Blackburn—from my in-law's house. On a bright day you can see Drum and Wrangell from my fishing spot, but it's been rainy and gauzy for so long I've forgotten what a bright day looks like.

Beyond that, anywhere you stand in the Copper River Valley was once submerged by ancient Lake Atna, a glacial lake formed during the Pleistocene (approximately 40,000 years ago) when glaciers from the Wrangell, Chugach, and Talkeetna Mountains converged and dammed the Copper River. This was around the same time that mammoths and woolly rhinos were running around up in Beringia in the Interior, and much of North America was covered by ice. Standing there fishing in such a place feels distinctly epic.

I don't end up leaving until the Samurai does. As I'm packing up, he comes by with—no fish. He stops and gives his two-fingered wave again. Then he speaks.

"You do any good?"

I gesture toward the fish on my stringer. "Oh, just the one."

"Better than me," he says. There's amusement in his voice, and I can't help but think he looks about as happy as a man can. Then: "You end up getting any yesterday?"

"Naw, it was a slow morning."

He cracks a grin and heads back up the trail. "Well, I guess I'll see ya tomorrow."

Back at home, I sharpen the fillet knife and set to work. I'm joined by Poppy the farm dog, an Akita/Pyrenese with a taste for raw salmon eggs even though they make her puke. We fillet the fish carefully because we have the time. I resolve to make sashimi with it. She gets a liver.

WEDNESDAY IS EMMIE AND MY OFFICIAL TWO-YEAR ANNIVERSARY. I get a little female sockeye. Around me the overcast skies evaporate and the Klutina is stunning there in the sunrise. It's just me, the disquiet of a river fighting toward the ocean, and the shrieks of juvenile bald eagles. I can finally see Drum rising over the trees, all twelve-thousand feet tall, and Wrangell (just over fourteen thousand) shrouded in elliptical clouds. Both are so white with glaciers and new snow that they look hot. The Samurai beats me per usual.

About six o'clock, another party of anglers come wandering down the path. It's led by a guy with a crackly old farmer's voice and a white beard, trimmed short.

"Back at 'er again, eh?"

"Yes, sir."

"Do you drive the blue Dodge?"

"Yes, sir."

We all recognize each other by our vehicles now. They have a white Ford.

SALMON HAVE ALWAYS BEEN OF GREAT INTRIGUE TO HUMANS. We know their story because we know their end; it's the one thing we still have in common aside from gill slits in fetal development. We're all swimming up some crazy river and at some point along the way, young or old, late or early, we die and rot into the silt. The really sobering thing is that death is the salmon's magnum opus. They swim around getting fat in the ocean for years sculpting themselves into efficient commuter vessels, then one day evolution calls them home and they follow olfactory signals to the streams they were born in. They put all that time and all that effort into mating just once, and they have no idea if they were successful or not before they expire. Billions of eggs will be eaten by other fish of the river; billions more will simply bleach and dissolve. It's been estimated that only two percent of salmon hatched make it to adulthood. I think I'd like to die for slightly better odds, but if we all must do it anyway, I guess it could be worse.

Thursday morning passes and I catch another hen. The Samurai gets one, too.

It's Friday, and I'm standing calf-high in the water early in the morning watching the currents gyrate and fold into faint hallucinations. I start to feel disembodied, floating away from myself like a helium balloon, watching it all happen from above.

You're strung out from the days on end of getting up at four. You take naps in the windy afternoons when the river is choked with fishermen. You sleep like a tree. Your hands ache and sting with the same casts, the same knots, the same cuts of braided line and fillet knives. Your brain starts to feel tenderized—jellylike—and in a moment of false brilliance you realize sockeyes aren't the only animals the Klutina makes zombies of.

By six I catch a nice buck, and by eight, there's a small hen added to the stringer. I don't dare hope that I'll get a full limit, but if there's a day it'll happen . . . it's today. Later I foul-hook a long-nose sucker which intrigues me. This river is swarming with life, but you can't see any of it. It's as unknown as the bottom of the ocean.

The white Ford group passes behind me ("Back at 'er again?"), and I start thinking about going home. Tuesday's salmon has been in the freezer long enough that I can thaw it and cut my sashimi. Just as I'm about to leave, the Samurai comes gliding down the trail. He stops, a pair of dime-bright salmon dangling from his hand.

"Got a couple, huh?" He's looking at my stringer.

"Yeah, they picked up a little today. Looks like you did all right."

"Got these two right off the bat, then I kept fishing just to fill my limit." He grins. "Guess I'm cursed."

Him and I both. I pluck up the courage to ask what's been intriguing me all week. "Do you live around here? You always beat me to the river."

The Samurai comes closer, the dead fish wobbling in his fingers. He has icy-blue eyes and a shadowed face. "No, we're from Fairbanks. We're staying over at the campground. I usually get here at one in the morning just to beat the crowds. It's nice to get out—things are quiet and it's just me and the river."

Any thought I had of potentially beating *him* here is dashed, and my respect for him only grows.

"I'm John, by the way," he says.

"I'm Joe." Simple names for simple fishermen. We shake hands despite the global urging for social distancing. If there was ever a handshake to break pandemic protocol for, this is it.

"You gonna come back this afternoon to try and fill your limit?" he asks.

"Naw, this place is a zoo in the afternoons. You?"

"Naw, I'll probably just go take a nap in the camper," he says, cracking a boyish grin that's made peace with the world and most everything in it.

We proceed to talk about whatever drifts into the conversation: rafting the Gulkana, dipnetting (I tell him I'm going on Sunday), smoking salmon, yarn flies, that kind of thing. He remains just John—I don't get a last name—and I don't find out what he does for a living, but I do find out that he's just recently retired from whatever it was. The image of him exploring the state with a fishing rod and napping in his camper during hot afternoons comforts me. Perhaps because I can see myself doing the exact same thing in a few decades. Finally, I get the feeling that I've kept him lingering too long.

"I'm sure we could talk for hours, John, but I suppose I'd better let you get on with your day."

I tell him that he won't see me until Monday on account of the dipnetting crusade. He groans and then smiles at me.

"I wish I could go with ya."

I DIDN'T MAKE IT BACK ON MONDAY. OR TUESDAY.

It wasn't until Wednesday morning that I was able to fish the Klutina again. Turns out I got a flat tire somewhere between Copper Center and Chitina, and by Monday morning the truck had a sad lean to it and the tire was squashed like a rotting watermelon. A farmyard nail was the culprit. I had to wait for Emmie to pick up a spare for me in Anchorage, and it wasn't until Tuesday night that I got it replaced. I had the sickening feeling that John and his wife would've gone back to Fairbanks; that I'd drive down to the bridge in the gloom of sunrise and the place would be deserted. Still, I hoped. If the Klutina teaches you anything, it's that.

Four a.m. and I was up, back to a routine that felt as coded as riding a bike. Make the coffee. Start the truck, grab the thermos, pee in the gravel behind the woodpile. Pour the coffee, drive down the Richardson, wonder if the run was petering out, wonder if the mosquitoes were bad, wonder if the Samurai had got his limit yet . . .

But there was no Samurai. His little turquoise rig was gone, and it was the first time in my life that I was disappointed someone didn't beat me to the river.

# EIGHT: DIPNETTING

*"The first black eye I ever got in my whole life was from a dipnet."*
—Anonymous

DIPNETTING IS AS ALASKAN-AUTHENTIC AS GRIZZLY bears and glaciers, and it's as near to the efficiency of commercial fishing that I think the average person should ever be allowed to get. You 'fish' with a three- to four-foot-wide net on a handle between six and fourteen feet long. You can sweep these nets from shore, hold them in an eddy and wait for salmon to tumble into them while you sip from a flask and watch for bears, or drift them from a boat with equal success. It's highly productive (I've heard of entire families catching sockeyes at a rate of a fish every thirty seconds), which is good because it's the only way you'd ever catch anything in the silty artery of the Copper River. That and in this state, salmon is a staple right alongside moose meat and craft beer. Dipnetting is allowed on a limited basis elsewhere in the state, but on the Copper it's the ultimate.

There's a dangerous ring to it whenever someone says they're going dipnetting on the Copper. Between its impossibly murky flows to its whirlpools the size of gymnasiums, to the sheer cliffs it has cut through ancient volcanic mudflows, it's a titan of a river that claims several human lives every year. I once watched the river swallow a truck, along with the EMT vehicle that was attempting to rescue it.

When I first dipnetted the Copper in late June 2020, I didn't really feel intimidated so much as curious. I'd heard about dipnetting and had seen the rabbles of vehicles bound for Chitina (the headquarters of dipnetting efforts) with nets and oversized coolers in tow, but I'd written it off as something I wouldn't do. Fish caught on rod and reel taste better, okay? But when a friend of mine named Peter, who's also a prominent professor of fisheries at one of the state universities, started talking about taking his boat down, I thought a little more about it. This was before I started fishing the Klutina, and I wasn't sure how my salmon stock would look for the winter. I also wanted to give some fresh salmon to my mother- and father-in-law being that they'd been gracious enough to take Emmie and I in during the whole pandemic situation. You let us live rent-free, I give you a few pounds of fish and sweep the kitchen every now and then.

I was fishing the Klutina one morning when I got a text from Peter:

Flows on the Copper look good. Meet upstream of bridge at 8 am Sunday.

Roger that. Now I was attached to this thing, as was Sean, a former co-worker but still good friend of mine. My next order of business was buying a dipnet permit, which cost all of fifteen bucks and gave me a limit of twenty-five sockeyes as head of my household, plus ten for Emmie. I know; it sounded a bit boggling to me at first, too, but then you realize that the sockeye runs are something like a million strong on an average year, and in terms of fisheries management, harvest by sport and personal-use fishermen is negligible.

My final (and crucial) to-do was finding a dipnet. My father-in-law had apparently dipnetted in Chitina before, but the only relic of this history I could find was the net itself—a pitiful hoop in the back corner of the garage with no handle. I went to Plan B, which was to borrow one from another co-worker in Fairbanks, have Sean haul it down for me, and compensate the co-worker with some vacuum packed salmon and Sean by filleting all his fish. Barters like that go on every day in Alaska, and usually they're far more outrageous.

If you're a fisherman, Peter is the type of friend you want to have. He's been in Alaska and studied its fisheries long enough that if he hasn't fished a certain place, chances are he knows someone who has or has at least read several research papers about it. He's an eternal well of fascinating and useful information (a fish's gill plate is called an operculum, for example, and Newfoundland is properly pronounced by rhyming it with 'understand'), and I make it a priority to ping him about my angling curiosities whenever our paths cross.

He meets us at the boat launch at 8 a.m. on the nose with his wife Donna, son Finn, and new yellow Labrador puppy named Tutka. We exchange the obligatory pleasantries and I tell him about the fishing on the Klutina, then we load all our crap in the boat and shove off.

"You're gonna want some rain pants," Peter says, looking at my bare jeans skeptically.

I *thought* about bringing rain pants, but you know how that goes. "I *thought* about bringing the pistol," is probably the last thought of most bear-maul victims.

Above the Chitina bridge, the Copper narrows from a winding, braided delta to a single current freighting past fish wheels and cliffs. Below, it widens out again and is joined by the broad

Chitina River which drains thousands of Wrangell glaciers. Peter revved the engine and flung us downstream.

It was essential that he relied on his boat's sonar feed to gauge depths. The Copper is so silty that you can't tell whether you're in six inches of water or six feet until it's too late. Huge gravel bars sprawled along the river's tumultuous middle, and mere feet from the shore on which recreationists stood and waved at us, it could drop to fourteen feet. The air was heavy with rain, the sky smoldering with mist. Gradually, the hills and mountains creeped inward, the cliffs of ancient volcanism got steeper, and the Copper narrowed against its will.

Huge upwells and whirlpools churned as though boiling. Millions of pounds of water struck rock and were pushed back. My mind was filled with one succinct thought: if you fell in here, you'd be screwed.

Around us the cliffs rose like reptilian backs; primordial giants with trees growing from their spines. Streams fell in weightless threads from high above. Against the walls of sheer rock, you would occasionally see a bright-colored rope dangling from an unseen tie-off. I might've thought these were for rock climbing given the pitch of the faces they were anchored to, but in fact these were tie-offs for dipnetters.

My guts squirmed. A few ropes were unmistakably broken.

I TOOK A DIPNET HANDLE TO THE LEFT EYEBROW, with enough force to draw a significant amount of blood, several minutes later. I had pieced together two aluminum handle sections to make one fourteen-foot net arrangement, and as Peter gunned it to get above our drift zone, the net caught in the water and sent the other end whipping into my face with the force of a Little League swing. Yes, I saw stars, and yes, I liked the idea that I had now paid in my own blood. To my own credit, I managed to catch the net, and it wasn't long after that I netted the first fish.

Dipnetting still seems a bit bizarre to me because the only connection I've ever had with a fish is through a hook and line. Peter would motor up above a particular run, then he'd let the engine idle, and we'd float down with nets held perpendicular to the riverbed (and opened downstream to catch fish as they swam *upstream*). You want to have your net hovering just over the bottom, so occasionally you'd strike rocks that could feel eerily like fish bumping into the net rim. Keeping the net straight against the relentless current was hard yakker, let me tell you. The first salmon I netted sent voltage straight up the handle, and I yanked the net upward hand over hand as though pulling anchor. It turned out to be a king salmon of twenty pounds, and being that king retention was prohibited, we flipped it out of the net unharmed. Later in that same drift I brought in the first sockeye, which Finn was happy to whack over the head and Tutka was happy to lick.

As Peter said, once the skunk was out, the fishing became predictable. I got the illusion that dipnetting was like clockwork, but I realized later that it was only because Peter had years of experience. It can be as eventless as musky fishing if the run is off or you're in the wrong spot.

Sean went through a period of lost fish where he'd get them to the surface and they'd tumble out and Peter would spew expletives, but eventually he started bringing them in hand-over-fist, as it were. Peter's boat was probably too small for three of us to be netting at the same time (Sean front portside, Donna starboard, me in the stern) with a fifth-grade Finn crawling around on all fours whacking fish and throwing them into the cooler and a Labrador puppy sleeping beneath the engine console, but it worked out. Before any of us really knew what was happening, we had half of a sizeable cooler loaded with salmon. A few of my highlights included netting a double of a sockeye and a fifteen-pound king (released), as well as getting a forty-some pound king that hit the net like a runaway firetruck.

Another thing about dipnetting is that you don't have time to wear fish down. If you do it right, they should be in the boat within seconds of hitting the net in the first place. A forty-pound king with his tanks full is a manic beast, and I couldn't help but recall stories of fish this size and larger breaking people's legs—or else knocking them overboard entirely—as they flipped rogue around a boat deck. We managed to untangle it without injury, and it surged away as though nothing had happened. I said to Peter:

"That's the kind I'd like to get on a fly rod."

We were joined in the drift zone by two charter boats, which were basically mobile meat-coolers with six to eight high-paying customers packed on deck like sardines. They played music, hollered like rednecks on Independence Day, and were otherwise obnoxious enough to drive us off after a few hours. We crossed the river and anchored up on a sandy beach, where we indulged in peanut butter cookies and smoked salmon.

By that point, Finn was covered from head to toe in fish slime and fish blood, but he took it with all the grace and amusement that a ten-year-old could—that is, grinning from ear to ear. He'd really honed his technique of clocking fish over the head and ripping out a gill to bleed them.

Peter is a lot like me in that we both get fidgety during breaks from fishing. Even if we're famished and dog-tired, and even if we're discussing something mutually interesting like Gulkana steelhead, we still just want to get back at 'er. After a few minutes of standing idle, he started kicking at the sand. I did the same.

Soon we were back on the river, roaring against the current and watching the canyon glide by. The cooler was so heavy that I had to sit across from it just to balance things out, and the engine groaned under the new duress. There was one last drift that Peter wanted to try just on the upstream side of the canyon. I was content to keep fishing, despite my aching muscles and jeans that now felt like eel skin, but Sean had a six-hour drive to Fairbanks and wanted to understandably call it quits soon. The new spot was a featureless gravel bank, but it turned out to be the most productive spot of the day. In just three or four drifts, we must've hauled in over a dozen sockeyes. A walk-in guide and his two clients were standing chest-deep, and from the looks of it they met similar success. Sean must've had the hot seat because Finn couldn't get them out of his net quick enough. We called it a day when we literally couldn't fit another fish in the cooler.

BACK AT THE BOAT LAUNCH, IT FELT ODDLY like time had been standing still all day. The sky was still the same shade of aluminum, the wind still screamed like a witch, and the river hissed with a gazillion particles of ground bedrock and glacial waste. Peter and Sean clipped tail fins per the regulations, and I divided up the catch evenly between our three coolers. By the end of it, we counted fifty-nine fish in all (and that didn't even include the kings or the sockeyes Sean lost or the dead fish that Finn accidentally threw out of the boat). It was one of those pleasing days that you never thought would happen and therefore only imagined. But then you kind of pinch yourself, realize that your eye is still swollen from its slugfest with a net handle, and that your truck is sitting a little lower on its shocks because there's a hundred pounds of salmon in the back.

Sean and I returned to the farm, where I filleted fish and he hosed them down and we saved the roe for his wife, Yoshie, to make a special Japanese dish with. It was late by the time he left and by the time I showered and went to bed. My body felt like it had barely escaped the Coliseum, and images flickered through my head containing broken ropes, maelstroms of frothing water, and muscly shapes folding themselves against nets before the crack of Finn's mighty bat made things go black.

I woke up with blood on the pillow from where my eyebrow leaked.

# NINE: A FULL LIMIT

I RECENTLY HAD A MORNING OF SOCKEYE fishing that was so perfect I'm still wondering if it actually happened. The very next day, somehow, was even better.

It was the birth of July, a month marked with hot, dry days and a general antsiness brought on by the passage of solstice. If you pay close attention and prescribe to the doctrine of pessimism, you can tell that the days are getting shorter as they plunge toward inevitable winter. We still have 22 hours of daylight left, give or take, but still. Summer, like oil and gold, is a commodity that Alaska can never have enough of.

I was up at sunrise with a newly changed and much-too-expensive tire waiting for me on the truck. It'd been a few days since I'd fished the Klutina, and that was enough to make it seem like an exercise regime I'd given up on. The bridge was deserted when I got there; the trail was quiet and cold, and my footsteps barely registered on the damp earth as I followed the whims of a thousand clomping boots that came before me. The path winds through dense riparian woods which muffle sound and clear the mind and swirl with smells of rain, decay, and age, then it opens into a stage of new growth where the river has changed and left a sandbar to be overtaken by willows, birch, and fireweed. It's close to this transition that I fish, and I duck down into my spot (big enough for one fisherman by design) and set my thermos on the bank. The air has an ancestral sting of winter within it, and I can feel it tingling in my fingers as I prepare rigs.

Prior to then, I had yet to catch my full limit on the Klutina, which is typically three sockeye salmon per angler per day. I'd gotten close on a few occasions with two, yet the hat trick was still eluding me.

The first cast is clunky. I realize the water level has dropped about a foot since I was here last. My weight is striking hard against rocks, so I clip off some lead and try again.

Most of the time, you get sockeyes about halfway through your drift, right as the line swings around to about forty-five degrees downstream. I let the rig swing all the way down, and as I was reeling in to have another cast, something wrenched on the rod and I was attached to a salmon as furious as a badger. He ejected from the water in sidewinding glory, then just as he came down the line fell dead. My immediate prognosis was that I hadn't set the hook hard enough—or really at all. Sockeyes aren't supposed to chase down flies.

It didn't take long to hook another and land it this time. I don't think I'll ever get over the excitement of battling Klutina sockeyes. I'll be forever cursed to the wide-eyed, open-mouthed, mindless-babbling trance that comes with witnessing them in the flesh. Chasing them over the last couple of weeks had become a vice and hooking them had become an injection of something euphoric. Like any potent street drug, the dosages did nothing to quell my addiction; they only served to feed a hungry and endless loop that led to nirvana, but one I knew was soon to be followed by windswept rock-bottom. The salmon run does end at a certain point.

I managed to keep my head screwed on tight enough to catch two more fish and lose several more. It was all I could do to pass college calculus, but that meant I had a full limit for the first time all summer. I drove home like a kid reeling with the angst of first love. It was only six o'clock, so I had time to fillet the fish and make fresh salmon cakes for breakfast.

Right when I started fishing for sockeyes at the tail-end of June, Emmie and I established a deal that if the fishing was 'hot', I was supposed to call her so she could come down and fish, too. Even if it was four in the morning. The last time Emmie had been sockeye fishing, we "knocked 'em dead," as they say, so I knew that whatever I called her for had to be damned impressive. Up to then, I'd only really had one solid day that I felt warranted a phone call, and she slept through it. It was just as well because the fishing had petered off anyway.

But the day after catching my first full limit of the season, the fishing was so good that by four a.m. I had a fish on the stringer, three more lost to my name, and the line was ringing to Emmie's cell phone. I could imagine her groaning from the bed and cursing my name, but hey, she agreed to the deal without coercion or bribery. She likes catching sockeyes as much as I do, it's just that she requires stronger odds to come down here and snag rocks for a morning. Yet again, she didn't answer. I sent a text saying something along the lines of, "The fishing is pretty darn good," and I'd hoped that she knew me well enough to understand just what that meant. A rare few things in my life are 'pretty darn good'—among them fresh margarita pizza, Mom's coffee cake, fall trout fishing on a certain tributary of a certain river, and Denali Brewing's Twister Creek IPA—so for me to classify something as such is about as solid as an investment in Amazon.

*Oh well*, I figured, and I went back to fishing. *Her loss.* Of course, because I had called her it started to slow down and I didn't hook anything for about an hour. It was about then that this skinny old man came hobbling down the trail.

"Mornin," he said.

At first the image of a skinny old man held out, but then I realized he was wearing a green jacket just like one I had, and that he had a distinctly feminine face and a ponytail the same color as my wife's. Then he went from a 'he' to a 'she' and from a skinny old man to Emmie herself.

Quite pleased with herself having tricked me (if only fleetingly), Emmie set her coffee down and got right to work. She approaches sockeye fishing with an assembly-line efficiency, which is something I feel I can learn from given that I waste entire fortunes of time and money on fish that may or may not exist. That is to say that if she doesn't hook a fish in ten minutes, she's second-guessing her decision to come all the way down and starts talking about going home. I think it might've taken eleven minutes for her to hook her first fish of the day (in which time I'd caught sockeye number two).

I get far more excited when Emmie hooks a fish than when I do it myself. And she certainly doesn't keep it quiet, so I know about it as soon as she does. The first thing I knew was that she was hollering something from downstream of where I stood, then she entered an attack stance, and I watched a lithe shape dance through the air and splash back down. Her shoulders dropped like an anchor and she faced me with a scowl. The salmon had thrown the hook.

She went through a pair of hooked and lost fish before she landed one. I had completed the day's limit and was fishing, per her instructions, so that we could always have two rods in the water. (Efficiency, I'll tell ya). The idea was if I hooked one, I'd hand her the rod and would otherwise be available to unsnag hooks and tie new rigs if need be in the meantime. I was in the midst of tying a flawless Palomar when she whooped in surprise, then I heard the punctual crunch of her boots charging down the gravel bank.

She played the fish as though she did this every day, and true to what you'd expect it turned out to be the biggest sockeye I'd seen all year, fat as a weaner pig and bright as a nickel. I was glowing with pride by that point, stunned into silence and inaction by the perfect morning that was playing out around me. A troupe of seagulls swarmed overhead hoping for fillet scraps, but I had to inform them that we cleaned our fish at home where there was a hose and Ziploc bags, and they'd have to inquire elsewhere. By then Emmie was on enough of a roll that she landed her next fish unceremoniously, and the capper to her limit came when I hooked a nice hen and practically threw the rod down to her.

Now, a stringer full of two sockeye limits isn't an insignificant amount of weight. By my best estimation, it was somewhere between an empty pony keg and a sack of reindeer feed. We took a few pictures with the fish all strung out between us. I felt a little smug when people walked by empty-handed, but hell, we'd earned it. And just how often do you get the chance to take pictures like that with your lovely wife?

By then the morning was heating up into the kind of July day that Alaskans cherish and take a million photos of to remember in February. I stood there trying to take a mental picture as you tend to do when things just go your way. The sun was atomic, the blue water of the Klutina rolled and crashed, and dawn shadows made the whole thing look like a storybook illustrated in acrylic. The love of my life was next to me and there was plenty of time to make more salmon cakes for breakfast.

Just then an old man, not skinny but not plump either, and certainly not wearing my green jacket, came tootling down the trail with the air of someone with all the time in the world. He slowed when he saw us, nodded at the fish with a smile, and took a deep breath.

"Such a blessing," he said, and he continued on his way before I could agree.

# TEN: WHEN I DIE, TELL MY WIFE TO BLAME JEREMY WADE

THE HIKE IS AS TERRIBLE AS EVERY OBSCURE REPORT I've read claimed it would be. In a way, this is reassuring. A 'get what you pay for' kind of thing—and I paid little to nothing to be here, save for sixty miles of fuel and just enough coffee to keep me alert at three in the morning. Two miles in and this trail is living up to every expectation it was afforded, those being "swampy," "miserable," and "no one in their right mind would do it." I'm soaked to my thighs, sore against the fifty-pound pack hanging from my shoulders, and I can't even stop for the slightest break because when I do, a flurry of mosquitoes zoom in for the kill like airborne junkyard dogs. If you put up with this kind of crap for five miles, though, you've got to be in for some good trout fishing.

I'm headed for the Gulkana Canyon. The Gulkana River itself is a tangle of three different forks that enter sporadically over its eighty-mile length and drain over two-thousand square miles, most of which is inaccessible except by raft or, I suppose, a bush plane. The river does parallel the road in its lower reaches before dumping into the Copper, but here it's wide and meandering and a better all-around bet for salmon than for trout. The upper stretches, however, are where the trout hide. These are special fish; the northernmost population of wild rainbow trout anywhere in North America, not to mention rumored to grow a yard long. I had been itching to give Gulkana rainbows a try for a while, but between the river's difficulty of access and my own occupation of waters further west, it had yet to happen.

My first order of business was deciding on a means of access. My brother-in-law Alex had a raft stashed in the garage, but Alex himself was tenured down in Haines and unavailable to take part in any adventures. I certainly didn't feel comfortable enough maneuvering a raft to embark on a four or five-day float of the entire Gulkana by myself, so that option was off the table until such time that Alex and his lovely wife Fran could cross the Canadian border for a visit. That left me one option:

Hoofin' it.

For all my angling life, I've been road bound. I've never taken a fly-in trip, and I can count the times on two hands that I've used a boat to get to suitable fishing water. I don't mind a hike, though, and honestly, the more arduous the better. I'm a firm believer in the equation that the harder a place is to get to, the fewer people it sees and therefore the more worthwhile its fishing will be. I combed old BLM records describing two trails leading into the upper river; one tracing a palsy signature through five miles of swamp to the Gulkana Canyon, the other crawling through seven miles of boreal and muskeg toward the confluence of the Mainstem and Middle Fork. The Haggard Creek Trail and the Middle Fork Trail, respectively. Eventually after much back and forth, I decided that the Haggard Creek Trail and the Gulkana Canyon would be my best bet, despite the pervasive recommendations that the trail should only be used in winter when the swamps were frozen.

So, there I was, slogging across floating rafts of muskeg at four-thirty in the morning. The only thing I can compare the experience to is tromping on the world's largest waterbed, and if you were to punch through the layer of vegetation on top, I honestly don't know how deep you'd go or how you'd get out. My feet were festering in a cocktail of swamp water. Thoughts pinged around my head imagining a bear around every corner and hoping no one slashed my tires while I was away. I passed ancient marten poles, bleached by the turnover of bright summers and biting winters. I envied whoever it was that operated this trapline and could run it with ease over snow. A mile further I found a set of wolf tracks.

To tell you the truth, I had almost contracted a terminal case of cold feet and not set out at all. It was the point where I'd done just enough research to suggest that the hike would be horrendous, it would rain all weekend, and the area I'd be fishing was so reputedly riddled with bears that hiking in solo was an act not far removed from suicide. Those are a lot of risks to take for a wild trout, especially when you've got a wife that you're fond of. Fortunately, Jeremy Wade saved me from wimping out.

THE ANIMAL PLANET SHOW *RIVER MONSTERS* became an instant hit with my brother Hank and I when it came out in 2009. It was hosted by a swarthy and tough-as-nails British guy named Jeremy Wade who travelled to the far reaches of the globe to catch, on a rod and line, these absurd species of fish that had been rumored to attack and kill people. There was the Goonch catfish of the Indian Himalayas, the piranhas of lore from South America, and the Goliath Tigerfish that looked like a product of Tolkien but was strikingly real as Jeremy Wade hoisted it from the waters of the Congo. He'd been chasing these fish long before he'd become famous enough to have a television show; in fact, he'd been doing it since his early twenties (about my age) when he'd work odd jobs long enough to set out on shoestring budgets to South America and return to family and friends grumbling about his lack of responsibility. Maybe he'd catch a fish and maybe he wouldn't.

In any case, his influence set me on many expeditions of my own, mostly for carp and catfish in the North Platte River of southeastern Wyoming where I grew up. But the real draw of Jeremy Wade was, and remains, the plain fact that he's a maniac. There isn't much he won't do for a fish, as later episodes and seasons and then autobiographies would prove, and that kind of anodized commitment transcends the stereotype of fishing as a mere hobby and puts it on a level of livelihood; maybe even on the pedestal of being a higher purpose. And why shouldn't it be? How is fishing any less of a valid calling in life than, say, selling insurance? I guess this is all to say that Jeremy Wade was the first person to plant these insidious ideas into my brain.

The main problem with Jeremy Wade becoming your role model is that, by all accounts, he should probably be dead by now. During his angling career, he's been in a plane crash, contracted a near-fatal dose of malaria, and been arrested in Thailand under suspicion of espionage, among other things. He regularly treks through Amazonian rainforests that give entirely new meanings to the word 'remote' and jumps into Himalayan rivers inflamed with rain for the sake of landing a fish.

I sat there thinking about the Gulkana Canyon long enough that my own worries started to seem pathetic, then I reached the ultimate resolution that, were he in my predicament, Jeremy would do it. He'd go. I suppose that's reason enough to suggest that when I die, you really should tell Emmie to blame Jeremy Wade because more likely than not it'll be because I did something a little too risky under a similar justification. Maybe I *will* be mauled by a bear (and I'll go down fighting if that happens). Maybe I'll catch some infectious disease or get shot for trespassing or just croak one day like an old farm truck. Who knows? The world is full of dangerous things, but as far as Jeremy and I are concerned, you might as well do one that lets you chase pretty fish and see the forgotten places of our world.

Your mind can tend to wander like that when your feet are planted as firmly as fence posts in muck, and you've still got a few miles to go before you hit the river. Despite my reckless abandon to be more like Jeremy, I had taken some extra precautions. First, I'd entered some waypoints from the trail into my GPS so that if I ever lost the path, I could find it again; and second, I borrowed my father-in-law's .44 pistol that was normally reserved for dispatching slaughter cows. I could feel it thump reassuringly against my hip with each step.

Even though I was packing both military-grade pepper spray and a pistol big enough to drop a black Angus bull in his tracks, it still scared the living daylights out of me when I stumbled upon a pintail hen and her brood of three ducklings. She exploded out of the tussocks and feigned a broken wing, and once the thundering of blood in my ears settled down, I gave her little family a wide berth.

I don't think it was long after that I heard it:

The restless noise of motion.

At first, I might've thought it was a highway—but then I realize it's too constant, too pure to be tires shuttling over asphalt. It's the river. It's the river thrashing itself through the one place I've come to see. It's the canyon.

I crash through the blueberry bushes. The trail begins to slope downward, leaving behind the bloated expanse of thawed permafrost and crawling over the submerged geology of ancient riverbeds. Sharp cries of gulls break through the static, then the gorge opens before me and I'm standing on a well-worn portage trail.

I'm quite sure my jaw fell open and I just stood there like an idiot for a minute trying to comprehend just what I was looking at. There are a few places like that in this world that are rare enough, hidden enough, and beautiful enough to make you feel like you're the first person to ever see them (even though you're most definitely not). Tubs and cauldrons of agitated water swirled behind tawny rocks, and on the opposite side of the river, cliffs forty feet high loomed like castle walls. This whole area was covered over by glaciers some thirty-thousand years ago, but when they retreated at the end of the last Ice Age, they left dense deposits of sediment and exposed monoliths of bedrock in their wake. The Gulkana proceeded to whittle its way through both over the next several millennia.

I hiked down to the beginnings of the canyon in silence, letting the chaotic noise of whitewater filter through me like a sieve. The water was a little high but clear as vodka, and I made plans to fish salmon fry imitations all the way down through likely holding water.

All through the canyon, the white kite-shapes of gulls and terns dipped and dove. They'd land in the middle of Class IV rapids and bob there like sloops, then they'd spring up again and plummet and emerge with sockeye smolts dangling from their beaks. I took care to watch where they hunted, for whatever water they careened over was likely to hide trout. It wasn't long before I caught the first; a little par-spotted fellow about seven inches long that fought with enough scrap to put a good jiggle in my eight-weight. While his purity and innocence were striking, I didn't come this far for last year's spawn.

My fishing became relaxed and unhurried, and I felt so free that much more would've made me sick. I had carried every possession I could need on my back. I had a goal, but moreover, I had a purpose as spontaneous and fluid as the river itself. I was my own planet, self-sustaining and mobile, and the galaxy around me contained all the stars of obligation that would be there when I returned home, but for the moment were lightyears away.

Down in the heart of the canyon I hooked my first proper-sized Gulkana trout.

It was in a seam where a furious rapid kicked around a rock the size of my truck, and this diversion left a strip of slower water tight to the bank. I clambered onto a boulder and swung a cast down through the fast water so that by the time the fly hit the margin, it would be a foot or so beneath the surface. A fifteen-inch rainbow darted from his hideout, ate the fly, and proceeded to fight like a fish three times his size before submitting to the net and my coveting eyes.

The beauty of wild trout will forever be indescribable, but that doesn't mean I'll pass up a chance to attempt. Looking at his lithe shape, I could tell not a scale was out of place. He was a deliberate creation, a devotion of time and skill as intricate as Etruscan filigree, and the red stripe down his flank and the daub on his operculum were the color of grapefruit flesh. He was beauty for beauty's sake; a stark antithesis to mankind's penchant for making things pretty to please a viewer. He wasn't there to please. He could've hatched and lived and died without anybody ever knowing it, beautiful for absolutely no reason at all.

I don't fish the place very thoroughly, more a cast or two in each spot before moving on. I've got two days to nitpick through here, and anyway, I want to see what it looks like further down.

Below the canyon where the cliffs end and the river stretches back into its normal shape, I come upon the first breach in my illusions of solitude. A pair of rafts are lashed to the bank, waving lazily in the current. I feel a charge of bitterness and then just resolve to leave them behind. The portage trail takes me right through the rafters' encampment, and I share a passing but inauthentic pleasantry with what I assume to be the ringleader.

Further downstream, where the path peters out into a web of faint bear trails disappearing into thick bush, the river splits around an island and I come upon a gentle stretch where dozens of small grayling are rising. Before long, even the bear trails are choked into the indiscernible, and it's about all I can do to fight through the tangle with a nine-foot rod and a swollen backpack that both seem to latch onto every branch in sight. There's a moment—several, actually—where I think that I should turn around and find a nice spot to make lunch. I could go back up to the head of the canyon and fish down carefully this time, making more casts than I know I need just for the sake of killing time. But then I start asking myself that dangerous question again—what would *Jeremy* do?—and the answer invariably comes back that he'd keep pushing downstream; infinitely fighting to see what was around the next bend.

By the time I do stop for lunch (a few cold bratwursts that I boiled the day before), I'm a mile further down the river with no new fish to my name. The only things of note I saw were a pair of ragged old sockeyes glued to the bottom of a deep hole, their bodies red as tomatoes.

The afternoon is still young, and my mind wanders back toward civilized spaces. I wonder what Emmie is doing and if she's left for Anchorage yet. She's photographing a wedding in Hatcher Pass near Palmer tomorrow, following a dream more productive and compensative than my own. I miss her. I start to think about what it would mean if someone *paid* me to fish in the same way they pay her to take pictures. I'm not sure I'd like it because I'd be governed by something other than myself. One of the primary draws of fishing is that it can feel as legitimate as employment, but it can just as easily become as functionless as a kid building mudpies in the driveway. The way it leans is up to me.

I become lost in the hours, back up in the canyon changing flies and locations without much reason besides having unlimited time to do so. Not one but two rafting parties float in from the anonymous waters of the upper river, and I just stand there and wave as they beach the crafts and start portaging gear. Being that I don't like having an audience, and it's getting to be that time anyway, I head up and find a patch of open ground and set up the tent and get some water boiling for coffee. My only pair of pants and shoes are still soaked with permafrost melt and mosquito larvae, and my waders have leaked right past the patches again, so I don myself with a pair of Hawaiian swimming trunks and forego fresh socks altogether. In this manner, I suppose I resemble a flagrant deadbeat or a hippie (a crime for which you could be shot in the county of Wyoming I grew up in), but then again, I don't really care. You tend to shed both sweat and dignity in this occupation. The trout don't care, either.

About then a middle-aged guy comes stomping by under a load of life jackets and spinning rods. He stops at my campsite and gives me a puzzled look. "Did you walk in by yerself?"

"Yep."

"How was the hike?"

"Eh, about as terrible as you'd expect."

He gave me another once-over, his eyes swallowing my bean-pole frame that was totally unarmed except for the pliers on my fly vest. My backpack was hidden in the tent. His face got real nervous. "Did you bring bear protection?"

"Something like that."

By then he had to have thought I was either as hardcore as they came, or else I was one of those kids that fell off a hayride head-first. Either way, he told me to drop by their camp in the morning and let 'em know which way I was headed so that if I didn't come back, they could come find me. I responded with "thanks" and kept silent the personal belief that I'm like a 4x4 vehicle in that, if I'm in trouble, there's not much else that can get me out. He returned to his portaging errands as I stood there barefoot drinking coffee.

That night I read Fred Gipson's *Old Yeller* and made one of those dehydrated, packaged meals of mashed potatoes. About then the rain started, and if we're keeping track it didn't stop until the next morning. It smacked the tent, pooled in the wrinkles, and streamed groundward like quicksilver. I was thinking about the river and just how hard it was to bushwhack once the bear trails had ended. Looking at the place from a satellite, the whole river looked open, accessible, *available* to me. With boots on the ground, though, it was impossible to wade and close to crazy to follow along the bank. Jeremy Wade or not, tight places like that along salmon spawning streams are where bear maulings always happen—and it doesn't matter if you've got bear spray or a bazooka because there's no time to deploy it anyway.

My gut told me to stay close to the canyon and fish it carefully. If I wanted to, I could just return home the next afternoon instead of beating the water senseless for an extra day. It might not be something Jeremy would do, but if anything, I figured, listening to my instincts was.

Old Yeller was just saving Little Arliss from a black bear, and the rain outside my tent had increased to the frequency of a Gatling gun, by the time I decided to go to bed. Trout swam above my head like shadows. My pillow was the shape and softness of a regulation brick.

Paul Schullery once said that calling fishing a hobby is like calling brain surgery a job.

I cannot pinpoint an exact moment, or even an advancing series of moments, when my interest in fishing went from one of passive amusement to an obsessive need to answer questions. (These questions, by the way, are still as unknown to me as the answers, and therefore just as alluring). I can only say that the regression has been getting worse and worse since whenever it is that it began. I suspect, though, that a strong surge in my own deterioration came as a result of hanging around the television with Hank on Sunday evenings. We did that more religiously than we attended church on Sunday mornings. At nine o'clock, provided the show was in season, there would be a swell of dramatic music and the black screen would melt into an image of a faraway river, usually with Jeremy Wade standing there with a fishing rod in his hand and looking like he was thinking hard about something. We'd then be whisked away on thrilling adventures and had to practically take sedatives by the time things were over and it was bedtime. During the ensuing weekdays, we'd usually wander down to the creek (or the river, if Mom would drive us) and try to re-enact whatever insane catch Jeremy had made. Typical halcyon days, though I could not see at the time just how deep and comprehensive my addiction was becoming. I was just doing something because I loved it; because it was there to do; because, amidst the swirling churn of adolescence, indecision, and misdirection, where everybody but me felt they knew what I *ought* to be doing, fishing started to feel like the one thing I was *meant* to.

It wasn't a job, and it wasn't a hobby. It was everything else.

I DIDN'T REALLY AWAKEN THE NEXT MORNING. I'd been tossing and turning and yanking the sleeping bag past my head all night, and I eventually decided to stop fighting it and make the coffee. It was around five. Plenty early to beat the other campers.

I ate granola drowned in milk, then I slid myself into cold, slimy waders. It was still raining when I crawled out and got to my feet, though the sky was glowing to the northeast. I remember liking the look of my shadow as I clambered down to the canyon, where the muffled roar of water escalated until I could no longer hear myself think. I was standing on the boulder from which I'd caught the first big(ish) trout of the day prior. Immediately in front of me was the giant rock around which a mammoth current plowed, and the two fans of whitewater it produced had to be Class III or better. A single Arctic tern divebombed from nowhere and entered the boiling space below the rock, then it emerged with a silvery tassel clamped in its beak.

And suddenly: *trout*. Everywhere. Their torpedo bodies gliding up, swallowing smolt, plunging back down to the floor of the cauldron. I wondered if they'd been there all along and I just hadn't seen them, or if they'd just appeared out of thin air as they seemed to. Other fish emerged in faster water, scintillating like copper, so big and so impossible it made my head ache. The sun had risen above the spruce-tops and was making the whole canyon glow. I knew I was amid a spectacle; I was standing there watching it and listening to it, I was caught in an undertow of the corporal and the unbelievable. All I could do was cast.

The smolt hatch turned out to be too good. There were so many fish in the water that my fly was lost in the crowd, and though my casts eventually reached the right places, they rarely reached them at the right times. Trout would come and go on their own fleeting schedules, and it seemed like every time I flicked a new cast, they'd flash once and be gone. The whole thing lasted twenty minutes, and I didn't even hook one. Maybe that was for the better.

Enlightened by what I'd seen, imagining trout in a million new places, I worked upstream. I crimped a bead of split-shot just above the knot to my fly, which made the whole arrangement cast about as well as a dumbbell but was enough to sink it in the torrential flows. By then the rafters were waking up, percolating down through the bushes and fishing with spinning rods from boulders strung along the canyon's edge. To my right I perceived the breach of a fish. My move upstream was automatic, the first few casts struck true, and I watched the trout chase one, ignore the other. I got above its holding lie, flicked a new cast and threw a mend midair, and in the trembling blink following entry I saw and felt the rush of the fish. Next thing I knew it was hooked, exploding like a steelhead, striking me with the gut-wrenching fear of loss that comes with hooking a big fish in fast water. *There's no way I'm gonna land this fish there's no way I'm gonna land this fish there's no way –*

It slid out of the water and crashed back down. It bulldogged below a logjam. It seared with the current, yanking first line and then backing, and I stumbled over myself in pursuit, remembering all too well the feeling of a slack line.

It's a dangerous thing to chase fish. Sure, there are the bodily dangers of drowning and bear-maulings and infectious agents and getting detained under suspicions of espionage, but even those end at a certain point. By contrast, who's to say that you won't get too close, that won't chase the fish just a little too far, that you won't climb the ephemeral reaches of thrill and elation only to lose what's most precious to you and fall flat on your sunburned face? The emotional tugs that come with hooking a fish leave traces. The angst of losing them leaves scars. The whole affair is dangerous as hell because, who's to say you won't hook yourself?

Somehow, I brought the trout to the net. She was thick, full-bodied, strong, as gorgeous a trout as I had ever seen. The northernmost strain of her kind. As I watched her pulsate there in the net, a sprig of ferality corralled just for the moment, I was so happy and dumbfounded that I could've burst. Yeah, I know. More than one person has told me, "Geez, it's only a *fish*," which I must cede is true. Maybe that's precisely why they're enough for me.

If I didn't have pictures of her, I wouldn't believe it happened at all. I let her gather the oxygen back into her body and get her bearings, then only when she resisted my fingers did I let her go.

THE HIKE BACK IS EVEN MORE TERRIBLE than every obscure report I've read said it would be. It's more terrible than I remember it being on the way in, because it's afternoon and not morning, and because I'm headed toward a highway instead of a river. But then again, as I slog thigh-deep through the new rain and watch mosquitoes the size of butterflies hover in front of my nose, I think I've come out ahead. This trail has delivered on every promise it's made, and even on a few that it hasn't. No one ever said I'd catch any trout.

There ain't much fuel left in the tanks by the time I reach the truck. My shoulders are swollen, and my legs feel as raw as wet leather. I'm, in a word, *haggard*, and I don't think it's a coincidence at all that the creek and the trail are both named for this feeling. I throw the backpack in the backseat and peel off my shoes and socks. I'll drive barefoot home.

It's just my luck that a bunch of men in hardhats are doing construction on the highway. Knocking down trees with excavators, standing around talking about horsepower and other crap. I have to knock on the window of a truck that's blocking the road out, and the gal inside gives me a similar up-and-down that the rafter did back in the canyon.

"We didn't think anyone was back there," she says, at least half apologetically. "No one in their right mind uses that trail in the summer."

I take it as a compliment and manage to figure out that I'll have to wait for the pilot car. She moves her truck and I sit there at idle with mine, staring at the streaks of mosquitoes on the windshield. Finally, I get back on the road, then when I reach service, I get a call from Emmie with the inevitable inquiry:

"How was it?"

I think for a moment, bubbling with all of a million things to say, feeling like I was gone far longer than I was.

"I'm kinda thinking about doing it again next weekend."

I like the sound of that, if only because it strikes me as something Jeremy Wade might say.

# ELEVEN: LITTLE STREAMS AND LITTLE THINGS

E VERYTHING IS 'LITTLE,' ALL THE WAY from the size 14 Goddard Caddis to the nine-inch wild rainbow trout it entices to the honey-colored pool from whence it enticed him. Today, 'little' is just what the doctor ordered.

I'd been chasing king salmon and larger rainbow trout for the last week. When I wasn't muscling cast after cast or staring at a big river and trying to figure out just where the heck fish would be holding, I was beating my head against an imaginary wall of concrete and wondering why two days of fishing had resulted in exactly one strike. It's humbling, sure, but it's also hollowing. Your arms get tough but your brain gets pureed. I started to forget that the whole point of fly line is to launch an otherwise weightless fly; something totally unlike the sparrow-sized cannonballs I'd been slinging into the big empty all weekend; something that, to be so perfectly weightless, must be *little*.

It was Sunday, and I was up early, and I took things slow

because the coffee was especially good, and the sky was especially blue. I watered the greenhouse, scratched the cat's chin, and helped my father-in-law clean up the mess of an overfilled water tank. I rolled out of the driveway around nine, which, by my normal fishing schedule, is the equivalent of sleeping in until noon. Further uncharacteristically, I wasn't even sure where I was going. All I knew was that I wanted a little stream, not necessarily but likely little fish, and a chance to cast a little dry fly again because I feared I'd forgotten how. The streams in the Copper River Valley where 'a little dry fly' constitutes acceptable tackle are few and far between—or at least they *seem* that way within the shadows of the well-touted salmon rivers—but I had a few aces in the hole. And if you don't cash in stuff like that when you're feeling a little glum, when do you?

The first was a little grayling and Dolly Varden stream to the south. It gets a run of king salmon and meanders through some thick bushy country that I was once told has the highest density of grizzly bears in the valley. A neat stream for sure; *really* neat when you watch forty-pound king salmon spawn in a trickle you could jump over. The only problem was that it was running high and muddy.

The second stream was one I'd never fished, which seemed as good a reason as any to check it out. It was rumored to be one of the better grayling fisheries in the area and I'd even heard rumblings that some rainbow trout haunted its pools. I guess in addition to seeking out 'little things,' I was looking for a reason to re-appreciate grayling, too, since they tend to fall to the bottom of my list most summers but are some of the loveliest fish on the planet.

I was using my six-weight which felt absurdly oversized, but I've found the action to be noticeably slower and a little easier to make short casts with. It's also a lot more delicate when setting the hook on lighter tippets. This is all, of course, a roundabout way of saying that I'd like to get a fiberglass four-weight—a devoted little rod to fish little streams just like this—but that's a conversation for another time.

Just upstream of the bridge there was a good looking pool where a set of riffles dumped into a cutbank. I was using a dry-dropper setup of an Adams Irresistible and a Pheasant Tail, and the plain fact that I was using insect imitations for the first time in months was immensely refreshing. I caught a handful of small grayling and gently unhooked them and let them swim free, watching their miniature dorsals wave like pennants. They were as innocent as schoolchildren, some so small they could barely fit their mouths around the hook.

I followed upstream against the current, sometimes splashing across riffles and sometimes inching carefully along deep runs cobbled with moss-covered boulders. My eyes stayed tethered to the stream, yearning to see around the bend, loving the idea that I could follow this water forever and just jump from pool to pool. Now out of sight (and earshot) of the bridge, I felt alone—not *lonely*, but singular, silent, and miniature. I guess there were a few things about it that could've been better. The water could've been clearer and not so tannic, the bottom could've been composed of smaller gravel to invite the spawning of salmon (and larger grayling and trout to eat their eggs), and you could get rid of that campground resort along the bank, to name a few. But then again that's all what makes this place so quaint. So imperfect. It's nothing more than a Sunday paradise.

Days later when I returned, one of the owners of the campground resort tried to tell me off for trespassing. He was wrong, of course, given the state's categorization of navigable water and the public's constitutional right to access it below high-water marks, but without yielding me the time to tell him so he rattled off a heretic speech about the possibility of me being a serial killer or a child molester or a bandit come to raze his property. I didn't tell him that I'd find better success robbing a soup kitchen than his ramshackle trailer house, but instead made my way back to the road and went home with a bad taste in my mouth.

Just past the campground—on Sunday, when the owner was still ignorant to my presence—I catch a wild rainbow trout. I'm as surprised as he is when he comes leaping out of the water, his nose punctured by a Goddard Caddis I tied back in April. He's all of nine inches, but the way his spots populate against his back like stars I can imagine him being much bigger. It's only after I release him that I realize he's my first wild Alaskan rainbow on a dry fly. I've only ever caught them on streamers or nymphs or egg imitations. It's a good reason to sit down and have a celebratory Snickers bar.

The grayling come readily with all the enthusiasm of fish trying to scrape by another long winter. Most take dry flies, while a few mouth the nymphs I've got tied to the hook bend. The largest is thirteen inches, sequined with scales as clean as aluminum. His dorsal hasn't yet developed into the long, fluttering canvas it will become one day.

I keep moving, past private property signs and old trailer houses whose residents would undoubtedly greet me with a shotgun.

Eventually I decide to go home, more in the interest of not overstaying my welcome than anything else. Places like this should be left open-ended and unexplored, if only to draw you back someday. Just before I clamber onto the bank and follow the dirt road to the bridge where my truck is waiting like a heeled dog, I make a tight cast to the edge of a shallow riffle. I'm not expecting much, in fact I'm not expecting anything at all. Something tiny eats the fly and it barely registers on the rod that I've hooked something. It's a little wild rainbow no bigger than my thumb.

I treat him as delicately as a butterfly, flipping the hook out of his mouth and holding him upright in the water. He's his own little solar system; par marks as bright as planets, a gentle red slash down his side like an asteroid belt. He makes me want to stay just a little longer in this wonderful little place, but then again, as he shoots out of my hand like a comet, that's a hell of a little fish to end on.

# TWELVE: PART OF IT

I T'S NOT VERY COMFORTABLE SLEEPING IN A TRUCK BED next to the spare tire and a cooler, but when it comes to Alaskan trout fishing on the road system, nobody said anything about comfort. I'm only minutes from the stream I plan to fish in the morning and can get there at first light (preferably before), and that's more than enough to compensate for the flat slab of metal under my back and the thunderous racket of semis freighting down the highway fifty feet behind me.

The plain fact is that the stream I fish is temporary. You could make that argument for any stream, of course, but in the fleeting measures of time that humans have, this one really is. It tumbles through beaver sloughs and runs parallel to the glacial waste of another river that drains some of the most formidable mountains in the world, twenty-thousand-foot Denali among them. Glacial rivers have a nasty tendency of altering course quite rapidly, and it won't be long before the river cuts in far enough to join with the creek and create a new and unfishable channel. The beavers and I stay busy worrying about this insidious change.

Somehow, though, I came along during the prime of my life while the creek was still intact. I don't quite buy into the grandiose idea that I was *born* to fish it, although I do take it as a sign to fish it all that I can.

In addition to some of the wildest rainbow trout on the planet, the stream hosts summer runs of all five Pacific salmon species; kings first, then sockeyes, then pinks (in even numbered years, which this one was), then chums, and finally, the cohos. For how small of a creek it is in terms of length, width, depth, and flow, it can be downright astonishing to see just how many salmon it supports. There are pools no bigger than the truck bed I slept in where, in late July and throughout August, you can find an army of several hundred salmon packed like cordwood. In September and October, you'll see a few ragged chums and cohos holding onto dear life with fungus eating away their bodies, while the sockeyes, pinks, and kings have washed up and begun rotting by the thousands. Whether through direct consumption of this decomposing tissue by fish, invertebrates, birds, or mammals, or through percolation of these nutrients into nearby plant species, scientists have found salmon nutrients up to seven miles away from their stream of origin. In this way, salmon spawning streams become vessels of life; paradoxical arteries in the eyes of an angler.

On the one hand, the stream can support steelhead-sized rainbow trout that may have once been anadromous, though through the millennia of evolution their life cycles have become restricted to freshwater. They can sit beneath overhanging trees, safe from eagles, and feast on a bonanza of salmon eggs and flesh for two or three months of the year. My good buddy Ryan Kelly was the one to introduce me to this stream, and on one outing we each caught several fish over twenty-three inches that were as fat as plucked chickens.

On the other hand, though, the productivity of the stream can make it both a pain and a danger to fish. Rather than fight the thick streamside bush, it's best to just wade the whole thing which, over the course of a day, can really put the hurt on about every muscle in your body. The other and more salient problem is the abundance of bears. It's riddled with both grizzlies and black bears who relish the chance to chase fresh salmon across the streambeds. You'll hear people say it's a stream that you should never fish alone, which was fine by me until Ryan moved away (a transgression I've yet to forgive him for). Now I feel like I'm playing with fire every time I fish it—especially when I start hiking in the dark.

It's around 4:30 the next morning, and it's at least light enough that I can see without a flashlight. My back is stiff from sleeping in the truck; my brain is slightly fried from that sleep being a whole two hours.

As I wade, I wonder how old the rocks beneath my feet are. God only knows for sure, but everything here just seems ancient. Like a land forgotten. Most of the streambed was left by the grinding trains of glaciers during the Pleistocene epoch between two million and eleven thousand years ago, which saw all of Alaska (save for a tiny region in the Interior) covered in miles of ice. Before that, most of the state was submerged by prehistoric ocean, broken by a smattering of islands and coral reefs that formed during the Cretaceous. I start to wonder if where I stand was once just such an island, and if any dinosaurs walked where I did. Paleontologists have uncovered hadrosaurid fossils to the north and west of here; entire swaths of footprints near Cantwell, a mostly complete skeleton named "Lizzie" in a quarry near Glennallen. Before long I lose myself in related thoughts and they only break when I hook the first trout of the day.

The trees swallow me as I go further downstream. Kingfishers ratchet from unseen lofts. I drift salmon egg imitations through likely-looking water, which is anything underneath bankside trees or behind breaks in the current. I catch a handful of smaller trout, some as bright as mercury dimes and others as spotted as jaguars. All of them are far stronger than you'd imagine a ten-inch fish could be. The thicker sixteen to eighteen-inch fish fight with a vigor that's inspiring.

In a few places I spot even larger trout hanging lazily behind pods of salmon. These are the "Holy Expletive" fish; the fish that, when compared to the big sockeyes resting nearby, are every bit as large. They're not interested in my beads, nor do they move for large streamers swung down in front of them. They're so close you could count their spots if you wanted to. Faced with these fish and cast after empty cast, it becomes easy to start personifying their behavior; to make feeble attempts to understand them. I move on in the bare consolation that there are just some fish you can't catch.

Part of the human experience is to envy the simplicity of animal brains. They're not bogged down by emotion or existentialism; they're not driven by ego or analysis. Humans are the only animals that commit suicide. Sometimes it's nice to shed our anthropologic trappings and pretend to be a trout. If you chase these fish long enough, if you suffer for them long enough, it becomes easier. The aches, the exhaustion, the dehydration all put a sharp edge on things; a contrast that makes whatever is in front of you vividly clear, while everything else melts into backwater. Your brain reverts to a shade of reptilian, focused and singular, and you don't just see the trees and you don't just hear the pings of birds. You *feel* them. You've got a lateral line.

There always comes the moment, though, when you remember that your brain and the trout's are separated by millions of years of evolution. You might as well be on two different planets.

DOWN AT THE MOUTH OF THE CREEK, three miles from where I started, I make a second breakfast of milk and granola. I haven't kept track of the number of trout I've caught, I just know that it's both enough and never enough.

The day is reasonably clear, and I can see the southern fringes of the Alaska Range. Last fall, I followed the creek all the way down to where it met the milky river, where trout were dropping down to spend their winter in the deep holes and struck bleached beads and flesh patterns with reckless abandon. This year, the channel has changed and where I previously caught fish after fish is dry, caked with dead algae, and punched with bear tracks. The fishing is good at the new mouth, though it must be the trout nursery because they're all so young and dumb that they strike at my indicator. An eagle watches me from seventy feet up as I trudge back up the creek.

I know I can never hope to understand this place as much as I want to. I'll never know the comings and goings of the beavers, the mink, the bears; just like I'll never totally understand the trout. All I have are guesses, educated or not by weather, time of year, lunar cycle, stream temperature—all human variables, and lots of them. I constantly estimate where the trout are. I wonder about the fox skeleton lying on the gravel bar like a macabre sculpture. I try to forget that I can only spend a few days a year here, and that the rest of the time, this place is as anonymous, wild, and forgotten as it was when it was buried by ice. I can never hope to fit in—to be a part of it—but I can forever hope to at least not be an intruder.

Back up in a pool where I caught nothing on the way down, just behind a pair of king salmon that must go thirty pounds apiece, I hook a big trout. The fish I've come for. My six-weight bends to the cork and the trout gives defiant headshakes that somehow convey both size and experience. She whirs downstream like a shooting star and then tires, and I bring her in as fast as I can before I let her slither right back. She's an old warrior with half her tail missing. This might be her last summer.

I go quickly on the way back upstream. Fishing in this place always seems to remind me how special the important things are (along with how trivial the rest of it is), and at a certain point I'm left thinking that I miss my wife and that it's been far too long since I've seen my mom and dad. Eventually I switch to a streamer for a change of pace, which moves two big trout out of pools that otherwise seemed empty. They follow it to my feet like muskies, but I can't get them to commit. Another chases it out from underneath a fallen tree and strikes, though his furious run throws the hook and I'm left wondering a good many things; namely, how big he was and how it would've felt to release him.

Being there, it's hard to imagine this stream as temporary. The cottonwoods and poplars tower like Cyclopes, the rocks sit quietly in the same places they've been since before I was born. I guess it's all enough to remind me that everything is temporary in its own way, that this happy coincidence of being here and being able to fish the stream as it deserves to be fished is as fleeting as bear tracks in the sand. You start to feel temporary and forgotten yourself at times like that.

Enjoy it while you can.

# THIRTEEN: DAWN

AUTUMN IS A TOUGH TIME FOR ME. Sure, it's my favorite Alaskan season by far and a welcomed change from summer which can tend to become cloying, if not nap-inducing, after a while. The salmon runs are finally petering out, the berries are sour, and just as you yearn for sun in the dead of winter, you long for that nostalgic chill of a fall morning. Then one day it happens. You feel the change, usually before you see it. Light receptors in the buried recesses of our brains sense the shifting angular quality of sunlight, our inner ears throb under new barometric pressures, and our collective psyche takes on an urgency that we can't explain. The forest turns dark and bare, the streams thin, the coyote's mangy summer coat grows thick as a mop, and we see reflections everywhere in a desperate land hanging on for dear life. Some people lament this end of summer and make taboo the hallmarks of approaching winter—the first freeze, the first snow—but I don't. My only problem with autumn is having so much to do and so little time to do it in.

On the one hand, the Alaskan trout fishing is spectacular between mid-August and mid-October. The fish are abundant, hungry, and usually fat from the protein of salmon eggs, and even their colors seem brighter amidst the gentle muted tones of the season. On the other hand, though, the grouse are beginning to stir, and the coverts are starting to wither into lanes big enough to swing a shotgun in. I'm a shameless neophyte in the world of upland bird hunting, so new that my wing shooting is downright terrible and I'm still so surprised by flushing birds that I rarely get a shot off anyway. But *something* about the handsome silhouette of a grouse strutting through vacuum-silent forest keeps me drawn to the occupation—and I suspect it's the same 'something' that drew me to trout and fly-fishing so long ago. My weekends become debates between donning waders or brush pants.

Aside from hobbies, fall really makes you think hard about your to-do lists. There is always more hay to put up or firewood to collect. For me, it means university courses and the start of the K12 school year, for which I am now a teaching intern. Everything is levitated in a matrix of ambiguity thanks to the coronavirus, and the things I'd been learning about teaching in a classroom over the last two years went out the window when my district decided to go all-online. It's difficult to connect with students via a conference call. It's difficult to inspire. But what the heck are you gonna do besides hold on and ride it out?

The 1957 camper that Emmie and I bought needed some attention, too. Our idea for the past several years had been to find an old 'canned ham' camper trailer (the kind that baby boomers hauled across America once upon a time) and convert it into a photo booth for weddings and other events. The whole wedding industry is one big boondoggle, though one that I have no trouble joining because my wife makes a significant portion of her income from wedding photography, and because I justified the purchase of some new waders this summer on account of a wedding video I produced. To have a wedding photo booth and complete our tri-fecta of entrepreneurship, though, I needed to finish said camper by installing the last pieces of the roof, building custom cabinets, and otherwise shoring up my improvised carpentry. By this point we'd moved into Anchorage, so we headed out of town on a Friday evening in late August with lumber trailing out the truck bed and a shotgun in the backseat.

THAT NEXT MORNING MAY HAVE BEEN THE FIRST FROST OF THE YEAR. The Tonsina River valley where I was hunting was swallowed by low, heavy clouds and driving down through it was like going underwater. Above the surface, the foothills of the Chugach Mountains ignited in the rising sun; below, the boreal was thick with fog. I got off the highway onto a chain of gravel roads that I'd discovered the year before while chasing Dolly Varden, where today the air temperature was a stinging thirty-three degrees. I chugged the last of the coffee and loaded a couple of shells into the 12-gauge and set out, crunching through patches of lowbush cranberries all silvery with frost.

Being so new to grouse hunting, I'm not familiar yet with their preferred cover. My hunting consists of following old two-tracks and stepping off occasionally to bushwhack when things feel birdy—that is, there are cranberries or rosehips in abundance and the trees are a mix of aspens, poplars, and spruce. Things felt birdy that morning but I didn't see a one. I skirted a tannic pond with a few mallards sleeping like ocean boats in winter, and down by an abandoned cabin I spooked a big old lynx who sprung away on feet quiet as moss.

I had my fly rods in the truck and thought about trying for some dollies in the little creek there, if only to get something familiar back in my hand after toting the strange heft of a shotgun. I decided against it. Just like with fly-fishing over a decade and a half ago, the only way to learn is to do it. Abandon the spinning rod and its conveniences. Learn to feel the backcast, watch how the current plays with a mended line, imagine the stream bed. Now I just

had to relearn a few things and completely learn others, like where
grouse hide in late summer versus early fall, like how to mount the
gun to your shoulder on a flush, like how to swing through a shot
and keep your head down. My last taste of upland hunting had
been the previous December when I slogged through four feet of
snow in Isabel Pass for ptarmigan. I found the birds, sure, but my
shotgun didn't.

Down the road I try a different two-track that's within sight of
another good fishing stop. I go along at a good clip, throwing the
gun to my shoulder for chickadees as they gambol around aspen
branches. I down all of them in my imagination. Now all I need is
a grouse.

In about a mile of searching, though, I find none. The trail I'm
on feels like it could keep going forever, and so do I, but then I
remind myself that I'm here to work. I return to the truck just as
the sun finally starts melting the cathedral of mist, and the woods
become washed in molten light. Around me, squirrels chatter and
knock spruce cones loose. A goshawk dips from branch to branch,
his wings the color of gunmetal. There is urgency in the air, the
feeling that a threshold has been crossed, that an hourglass has
begun streaming in sudden acceleration as the year tumbles from
one apogee to another. The transition from summer to fall, from
light to dark, is as fleeting and precious as a sunset, or as a dawn
just like this one.

I stop at a pond where there's historically been good trout fishing and tell myself that I'm not even going to fish. I'm just going to
look for rises. Nestled in a little hollow, the pond is sedated and the
color of sheet copper. Woodsmoke climbs from a tent site hidden
in the trees.

There it is. The rings of a rising fish. The sound, the sight makes
me hold my breath. Another, like a solar flare behind stars of twit-
tering no-see-ums. This afternoon I'll finish the camper roof and
tomorrow I'll hunt grouse at the end of my father-in-law's hayfield and I won't see anything but a young coyote that I manage to

call within twenty feet of myself, but right now, looking out onto a pond, and out into a season far too short that's just begun, I decide to grab the fly rod and try a few casts.

# FOURTEEN: POPS

MOST OF MY CHILDHOOD FISHING MEMORIES have one thing in common, and that one thing is one of my best friends in the world. He's 84 years old at this writing, the father of my father, and I call him Pops.

The first of these memories that I can conjure occurred on an atomically bright day in northern Colorado in the early 2000s. I want to say it was Waneka Reservoir down by Lafayette, where grasshoppers were trilling from thirsty grass and killdeers were screaming from their nests in the gravel. I recall many summer days just like that as a kid, but this one stands out because I was hoisting a whopper bluegill. (I would've been about five years old, so take 'whopper' to mean whatever you feel is appropriate for a five-year-old to define). Whether or not it was *really* that big was beside the point; Pops had said it was 'nice,' and that was enough for me.

Pops had a white single-cab Ford. I recall it well being that it was a stick-shift and I always had to sit in the middle and move my knees when he changed gears. My brother Hank was older and moodier, so I rarely—more than likely *never*—got the passenger seat.

We'd leave early on our fishing expeditions with Pops, often before dawn, which I hated at the time but now consider to be my modus operandi. Usually, the drives were long and took us down some horrendously corrugated gravel roads in the backcountry of Colorado or southeastern Wyoming. Pops would regale us along the way with tales of what he'd caught the weekend before, or he'd ask us about school or what we'd been up to, which we'd reply to with typical child vagueness and answers like, "I don't know." Pops was one of the few adults that actually challenged us on this; he'd ask, "What *do* you know?" and expect an elaboration.

The best thing about fishing with Pops was that Hank and I basically got turned loose. Those long drives are killer on restless boys' knees, and when the truck finally stopped, we'd blast out of there like a covey of quail. Pops, on the other hand, would turn as focused as a heron, and I think Hank and I could've wandered all the way to Mexico before he'd notice we were gone. That wasn't ever a problem though; Pops would spin tales of "them big ones" with just enough ambiguity and frequency to keep us interested. He managed to catch one of "them big ones" every now and then too, so Hank and I thought it best to emulate his persistence. He also brought the best snacks; the kind of junk food Mom wouldn't let us have in a million years. We'd sit there and spear gobs of nightcrawlers on snelled hooks and shove irresponsible amounts of Funyuns and Cheetos down our little throats and Pops would always be nearby, reminding us to "let it sit" whenever our fingers crept toward the reel.

TODAY I'M 24 YEARS OLD AND THINKING ABOUT those days spent with Pops as I head out on a fishing trip of my own. I'm 3,000 miles and two decades away. These days I fish mostly solo.

It's a bright day on Alaska's Parks Highway, so bright that I could mistake it for Colorado summer if it weren't for the black spruce picketing the highway and the view of Denali before me. Being Friday afternoon, the campgrounds are clogged with motorhomes, and being just after the start of some moose and caribou seasons, every pullout is clogged with trucks. Both start to get scarce the farther north you go, so that's where I'm headed. I decide to fish the stream near my selected campground in the interest of a reasonable bedtime; if I fished my go-to, I'd be there until midnight.

Where the creek meets the river, things smell fishy. A combination of wet sock and seafood. The pinks have shown up in legions as they do in even-numbered years, and I'm glad to see them on account of the fat trout I know tend to hang around nearby. The pink, or humpback, salmon is the unsung hero of Alaska—not much to look at (though handsome in their own drab way), but nonetheless indispensable in the survival of their natal streams. The females are pale and lithe, and the males develop humped backs so tall they become the shape of a cake dish. I pass a few on the bank, either dead-eyed and rotting beneath patches of fungus or sidewinding in their final throes. Their carcasses are corralled by bear tracks.

Sometimes I wish I'd grown up on a stream just like this. Salmon and ferns and seasons as binary as a light switch. Then I recall that Rawhide Creek (where I did grow up) wasn't so bad, either. Hank and I would catch creek chubs there so big and fat they were trout-sized, and occasionally we'd hook into leviathan carp that hauled us down the bank like barges. The creek was heaven for trapping in the wintertime, too. Raccoons scuttled around in the mud and muskrats lived in the slow pools and mink slithered for miles on end down the grassy banks. I chased after all of them. One time I saw a set of bobcat tracks, and another time while I was catching chubs on caterpillars, I saw a four-foot river otter come blasting out of the cattails.

Cue the touch of homesickness, and it isn't long before I'm missing Pops, too. The last time I saw him was over a year ago; the last time I fished with him is going on four. My family had come up to Fairbanks for my college graduation, and we spent an afternoon on a slough of the Chena River where Hank, Pops, and my dad all caught their first Arctic grayling.

It's hard for an Arctic grayling to not end up on a devoted fisherman's bucket list. Even though they're small (at least by the standards of trout), they're a lovely-looking fish and fabulously exotic. They used to be spread across Alaska, Canada, Montana, northern Wyoming and Colorado, and parts of Michigan, but with warming trends and human expansion in every direction, they're limited to just Alaska and Canada these days. There's a modicum of lakes and rivers in the lower-48 with healthy stocked populations, and growing up you'd occasionally hear Pops tell yarns about Colorado's examples. His eyes always took on a signature gleam when he talked about these mystical places, whether because they held grayling or giant trout, and, to his credit, we ended up fishing most of them. We never caught any giant trout (except for a granddaddy brown that Pops caught in one of the Hohnholz Lakes near the Wyoming-Colorado border one time), and we certainly never caught any grayling. Looking back, I'm fine with that; it was one of the greatest pleasures of my life to help Pops catch his first on Alaskan soil.

I fish all the way from the creek mouth to the road crossing with nothing to show. The afternoon is taking on the angled light that means it's evening, and that summer has finally, or prematurely depending on how you look at it, tumbled into fall. Denali fades behind purple haze.

I'm sleeping in my truck bed again. It's a little tight with a full-sized spare tire, a tote full of camping gear, and the odds-and-ends of my fishing outfit back there, but it works. I'm here for the trout; sleep and shelter are peripheral necessities. The campground is just a slab of asphalt, but it's the closest one to my favored stream so I take it without complaints.

A guy pulls in with his Jeep and asks me how the fishing was. I'm honest and he frowns at my lack of trout. Then he says he'll go fishing at so-and-so creek in the morning, and this sets my hackles up a bit because that's where *I'm* going.

"You camping?" he asks.

"You could say that. I just sleep in the back of my truck."

He gives me a look like I'm pulling his leg. "No way."

"Too much time to set up a tent."

"And you don't want to spend that time, huh?"

"Nope."

Not when there are trout to catch, anyway.

I'VE NEVER SEEN A PERSON HAPPIER THAN POPS when one of his grandkids caught a fish. He'd turn as giddy as a schoolboy and fetch his stringer from the pickup and start singing praises that made you feel as loved as a good dog. Hank and I would always hope to be the first, though it seems like often Hank struck first blood. He'd bask in Pops's excitement and I'd turn green with jealousy. Truth be told, I wasn't that good of an angler. I was twitchy, impatient, overthinking. A few of these curse me today.

That next morning after I crawl decrepit from the bed of my truck and manage to boil some coffee, I'm wandering down a creek in the dark and screaming my lungs out every hundred yards to warn any lingering bears. In classic Joe-fashion, I'm still searching for that first trout. My casts getting progressively more desperate with each pool that I just *know* has to hold fish.

Finally, around five-thirty, I notice a shape that seems out of place amidst a hole stacked with pink salmon. It's a rainbow trout, long and roguish, sitting in a pillow formed as the creek dumps under a fallen log. She eats on the first cast. I prepare myself for the fight of my life—these trout are notoriously scrappy—but she comes in like a drenched wool sock. At the bank I see why; she's old and haggard from spawning this past spring, a fish just holding on, too tough to die before the bounties of summer are over. She lacks the metallic luster of a trout in its prime, but she's still one of the prettiest animals I've ever seen. I feel a slight guilt at putting her through this ordeal, like taking advantage of someone dear, and I let her go as quick as I can. She sidles right back where I found her, darting side to side and swallowing salmon eggs like they're dumping out of a slot machine. Pops would've clapped me on the back for catching the first one of the day, then he would've called her a "nice one." For that matter, so do I.

Time pulls me downstream through the wake of lumbering grizzlies. Gravel bars are strewn like battlefields with torn salmon carcasses and the footfalls of heavy pads with long, draping claws. Most of the fish are still intact save for the heads. Bears love the brains.

The water, meanwhile, is restless with salmon. They lay scattered in the riffles and packed like muscle fibers in the deep, slow pools. Whenever I cross, the creek ignites. One salmon spooks and sets off a chain reaction as quick as gunpowder—soon, the surface is roiling in collective anadromous lust, generating waves that lap against the alder roots like heartbeats. Most of these fish are the tell-tale mud-and-white brushstrokes of humpbacks, with a few streaks of sockeye dotted in between. I see very few trout and catch even less (though one of them is a thick twenty-two incher).

Down at the mouth of the creek some hours later, I make a cup of coffee and sit still for the first time all morning. I'm staring off into the foothills of the Alaska Range, steadily inflating with questions, watching the wind on the river throw silt around in miniature sandstorms.

POPS APPROACHES FISHING WITH AN ALMANAC matter-of-factness. He always has. He doesn't care much for fish biology or the proper names of insects; to him, the best explanation for a day of no fish is that they just "weren't biting." Maybe the moon wasn't right. I've heard plenty of tweed-and-cane types trying to tell Pops the full Latin designation for various types of mayflies, and that a certain variation of gray was working well on whatever day it happened to be, or that trout were reluctant to feed on the surface in the bright sun and he should be fishing an emerger. Pops would act nice enough and let them finish their speech before holding up his leader and saying, "I just use this little Cahill fly." And usually, he'd proceed to fish circles around them.

Another thing about Pops is that he fishes flies quite often, though he rarely fly-fishes. He may have tried it once but found it to be more trouble than it was worth and has since resorted to casting flies with a spinning rod aided by a bubble float. Usually right after the same tweed-and-cane fellows would try to give Pops and Hank and I some education disguised as advice, Pops would press the button down on his spincast and fling his bubble a good two or three times the distance those guys were hitting with their fly rods. I mentioned the time Pops caught a Hohnholz Lake brown trout so big it would've made a fly-purist's hair curl. Years later when I started fancying myself as a fly-fishermen who *didn't* use bubbles, Pops would similarly whoop me with his tried-and-true method. These days I don't care who you are; you're never too good to fish a fly behind a bubble.

Sometimes that's easy to forget, though, especially when you start accumulating your own gear and ideals and before you know it, you're shrink-wrapped in Simms waders and you own a Sage and you know the difference between indigenous and wild and stocked trout (and that there *are* differences at all). The Latin designation for certain mayflies becomes prerequisite knowledge and matching the exact shade of gray becomes your crusade at the tying vise during long winters. You'll gladly fish an emerger if you have to because you've got a box full of them (though you're not so much of a Puritan that you won't fish a plastic bead once the salmon are in).

Once you get enough of those pretensions tucked into your hat, it can be difficult to imagine the trout as simply, "not biting." But given my lack of alternative answers, I sat at the end of the creek and finished my coffee and started to think "not biting" was as reasonable an explanation as any.

BACK UP THE CREEK A FEW HOURS LATER, where the sun has penetrated the woven canopy of a place I call the "Beaver Pool," I see more trout. Compared with the pink salmon, which can go all of eight or nine pounds, there's one trout that seems even bigger. Maybe it's my imagination, and maybe it's this tiny creek that I could almost leap over that makes trout seem disproportionately huge. Either way, I sit down and carefully rig a bead on lighter tippet and tell myself, "If she takes, she takes. If she doesn't, she doesn't." I'll give it five casts, then I'll watch the trout for a few minutes and move on.

It's difficult dropping a cast behind the pair of fallen trees, but that's where the trout is. Glued to the softened current. Below me, there's a heroic feed pile that several generations of beavers have been contributing to, and the creek has eaten out a hole that might be over my head. I think if I manage to hook this trout and she goes in there, I've got no chance of landing her. That's always the danger of fishing. Putting your heart out there raw and unguarded.

She takes on the third or fourth cast, and the only exclamation I can utter is a gasp. Off we go, the trout seeking cover in the handiwork of the beavers, me walking the tightrope of wrestling her out and not snapping the line like horsehair. My heart thunders, stops, I put some muscle into it and drag her out, and I know it's not my imagination anymore because she's right up against a big old male pink and she's even longer than he is. I get her to the bank, awash in relief. This is my best trout in several years; all of five pounds; six, even. And as incredible as hooking and landing her was, watching her go is even better.

ONE NOVEMBER WHEN I WAS SEVENTEEN, Pops came up for a weekend while my parents were away. I don't know if they didn't trust me to keep the house from turning to ashes, but I didn't care. Pops and I made hobo chili, watched *All in The Family*, and checked my string of raccoon traps down on Rawhide in the mornings, and one of those days we went fishing in the nearby Platte. It was cold as hell, but we caught a stringer full of the largest smallmouth bass I've ever seen.

Another time we drove all the way into Allen Basin in the Front Range of Colorado and fished all day and caught nothing. One time we drove all the way into Wyoming's Sybille Canyon only to find the road to the lake closed for construction, so we turned around and went home.

Fishing could seem especially functionless (and to an adolescent, *point*less) on days like that, but I figured if Pops could justify sitting around staring at water for hours on end or driving halfway across the state for the idea of catching fish, I could too. His past included a post-Depression-era leanness and a work ethic that left little room for hobbies. By the same token, though, Pops was always one to demonstrate that you shouldn't take fishing (or anything, for that matter) too seriously. In all the years and all the miles I've spent with Pops getting jostled over potholes or having my knees banged against the shifter, I've never once seen him get mad at a lost fish or skunked days or wasted gas or bad weather. It's only fishing, after all.

THE NEXT MORNING I'M BACK ON THE CREEK just as day starts to break in steely, Cimmerian light. The big female trout from the day before is back where I left her, which I'm glad to see, but today she's accompanied by two compatriots. They wiggle amongst the pink salmon like bad imposters. One is twenty inches—a gorgeous fish—and the other is as pale and long as a steelhead. I guess from his rocket-shaped nose that he's a male, and I start making tentative casts. He looks once and dodges the rest. I sit on the gravel bar because I like to think that's what Pops would do.

Ten minutes pass. An old man and his son come tromping down the bank and we exchange the pleasantries of anglers disappointed to see one another but at least happy to know we're not *completely* alone. They hoof on, bound for the mouth and what they hope to be some fresh cohos.

I wait some more, until I've breathed the air and the faint decay of salmon steaks and the first shedded leaves, until I watch the sun crawl through the canopy in rods as warm and bright as smelted gold, until I appreciate the trout from a distance rather than in my hand and begin to think that just seeing them could be enough. Then I get to my feet, sedated by newfound patience, as relaxed as though I'm sitting in a lawn chair with a bag of Funyuns in my lap. I cast, the big trout worms over, and his great white maw flashes once and he sizzles off like a runaway steer. I only know I've hooked him because the line goes with him.

3,000 miles and two decades from where it began, I'm attached to unbridled life. The trout plows under the log and for an ugly second, I'm not sure if we're still connected or not, then he comes out and I guide him toward the bank where I get hands on him and kneel there, feeling a dizzying swirl of euphoria, culmination, and nothing at all.

The rainbow is all colored up like he finished spawning not long ago, his belly the gentle red of rosehips and the stripe down his flanks as bright as a high-bush cranberry. He's got the gnarled kype of an alpha male with an attitude to match—this is one of "them big ones," the kind of trout that comes along only a handful of times in your tiny little life. He kicks out of my hand, the slap of his speckled tail etching itself into my mind like a fossil.

That trout becomes the only one I catch all day. I fish quickly but carefully, spooking armies of salmon, following a family of mergansers. I'm living a day that I'll look back on in twenty years and remember as atomically bright, desultory, and punctuated by one, spectacular fish. It's the continuation of a cycle as sure as the humpbacks returning to the streams they were born in; as trout spawning, growing old, and dying; as a towheaded kid hoisting a bluegill and having no idea that the illness creeping over him is terminal.

I'm halfway back to the truck when I see wet pawprints on the gravel. They lead to a pink salmon hen, still flopping, fresh scarlet blood oozing from a torn side. I've almost gone two days without seeing a bear here, but my hair prickles in that primal anticipation at knowing I'm about to.

Around the bend there are two of them. Grizzlies. They wade shoulder-deep amidst schools of salmon, and soon I see a third creep from the bushes. They're young ones, perhaps four-hundred pounds, still bearing the soft features that one might call "cute" if they weren't a hundred yards away in open air. I scream at them, but they pay as little attention to me as a kid ignoring a parent.

Then the big one comes out. I assume it's the matriarch, but when she looks toward me and rears up on her back paws, a full seven feet above the ground, I don't assume anything. I don't think anything. My mind races through an empty forest of the most basic of feelings:

Fear.

I scream at them again, louder, then a second time and a third and a fourth, growing manic and decidedly puny with my bearspray as they look toward me. Without warning, the big one turns and plods off into the ether of trees. The young ones follow. I stand there with my heart bucking like a wild horse for several minutes before I'm brave enough to move on. Then I start to wonder what Pops will say when I tell him what happened.

# FIFTEEN: HIDDEN IN PLAIN SIGHT

I WILL SAY NO MORE ABOUT THE CREEK THAN THIS:
It flows into a glacial river somewhere between Moose Pass and Seward, it holds Dolly Varden up to (and often surpassing) twenty inches, and if I threw a rock hard enough from one of the best runs, I could get it across the asphalt of a well-beaten road.

This is one of those special places, a small-stream gem hidden in plain sight where, as you hook and land fat dolly after fat dolly, you wonder why the parking lot is empty on a Saturday. Sure, it does get fished more often than I'd like to think, but it's also mysteriously devoid of the boot prints and scarred fish that otherwise define Alaska's roadside fisheries. In one direction you look out into a valley of mountains that could be a hundred miles from anywhere, then you spin a one-eighty and you're watching Nissans bumble past and runners wave at you from the bridge. You can either stand there like an idiot trying to figure out how and why this place isn't pounded to a pulp, or you can just enjoy it.

I move up and downstream in a stretch no more than a quarter mile long. The pink salmon are scarce, and I wonder if I'm early or late. Behind the few schools, though, there are impish Dolly Varden hiding in the gray mottling of cobblestones, and most come easily on beads or flesh flies. Down near the mouth, there's a run about as long as an RV that I meticulously fish and catch a dozen fish out of; two of which surpass the magic twenty-inch mark that make you stop and wonder if you should pinch yourself.

They're big spawning males with jaws so hooked they look like deformities. Their bellies are the pale orange of a western evening sky, their sides the emerald-blue of glacial ice. I've dreamed of catching fish this big and this pretty for a long time, and I won't say it was a culmination—but it felt like it. It felt like I was somehow cheating a system.

ALASKA'S ROAD SYSTEM IS THE MOST WONDERFUL PARADOX in the world. On the one hand, you have millions of acres of mountains and rivers, none of which could be accessed short of boat, plane, or boot leather without roads. Alaska has a total of twelve numbered highways, along with a tangle of old traplines and ATV trails that can pass for roads if you try hard enough. Of the state's half-a-million square miles, though, only about twenty percent is accessible by road, (and this twenty-percent is more than a four-wheeled mercenary can cover in a lifetime). On the other hand, these few roads can leave scars that grow like toxins spreading through a bloodstream. Bears get poached and left to rot, moose and vehicles have encounters that usually end poorly, and the halfway-decent trout were either taken home on a stringer ten years ago or are so hard-fished now that they've developed the skittishness of a spring creek brown.

Lest I sound like a petulant child about the whole thing, I wouldn't be much of an angler without these roads. I've been

known to put thirty-thousand miles of tire rubber down in a summer chasing fish, and while driving that much does show you a
few of the uglier exhibits of our species, it can also give you some
hope now and then. Alaska is still so big and grand and there are
still those forgotten little coves at the end of gravel roads, some
even near asphalt. It's just that now, in the 21st century of internet
headlines and angling debutant Facebook groups, it's less a matter
of catching good fish right below bridges and more a chess match
of trying to find and trick them elsewhere.

It's been said that there are no good anglers in Alaska, there is
only good fishing. I would've taken that as creed a couple of decades
ago, but I think today, if you're just a guy or a gal with a truck and
a handful of free weekends a year, you can't afford to be *bad* if you
really want a shot at decent trout or Dolly Varden or grayling. You
have to put in the research and the gladiator hikes; you have to
make good casts and put some thought into what you're present-
ing to fish and why and when; but most of all, what I take to be the
guiding principle of road bound anglers everywhere, you have to
keep your mouth shut about it.

That's part of the reason I duck when I hear another car coming
across the bridge. I'm heading back to the truck after those cosmic
few hours of dolly fishing, and the last thing I need is for someone
to see my fly rod and start to wonder.

This little creek is both as visible and as cryptic as the best
hole-in-the-wall Thai place you've ever been to. Part of its obscu-
rity comes from the fact that it isn't named, and had I not read
about it, I'd have thought it was just a channel of a particular
glacial river that flows through that country. The thing about
new creeks like this is that they're hard to bring yourself to fish.
What I mean is that it's difficult to make the time to fish them
when you've got a list of named and proven-to-hold-fish places
just down the road. You must abandon a sort of dogma and let
go of the handrail, and I don't know if it's the hardheadedness
of people in general, or the supreme thickness of fishermen's

skulls that makes it so difficult. Most of the time you end up getting some casting practice, maybe hooking a fly in the branches behind your ear and returning to the truck. Sometimes you catch a few fish and have a downright pleasant afternoon, and sometimes you experience some of the best fishing of your life like I did that morning near Seward.

I have found, though, that regardless of the fishing, these modest streams always find ways of staying with you. You slow down when you cross them, and even the ones you've never caught anything out of still just *look* so good. You remember intimate details about the places, like where the harlequin ducks like to sit, or how the air smelled like almonds as the creek carried it out to sea.

What I remember about Ptarmigan Creek, just up the road from my unnamed stream, is that it sparkled. It sparkled white like champagne, it sparkled red with all of a hundred sockeyes. There were about two dozen cars in the parking lot and in a half hour's fishing I ran into seven other anglers, yet the place still sparkled. I caught two rainbows so young they still had their parr marks, and the biggest trout was something like thirteen inches. Not the best stream I'd ever fished, but certainly not the worst, either. Watching sockeyes flow upriver like spilled paint has to be one of the most quintessential Alaskan things you can do (short of watching northern lights or riding in a dog sled, maybe), and I could've sat there and done it all day if there weren't more streams to fish. Walking back to the truck, passing two dozen cars and then some, I decided this might just be one of those places worth keeping in my back pocket, if only for the hope of a lazy Saturday to return on.

Next was Quartz.

If the creek near Seward was as close as I could get to virgin roadside fishing, Quartz, so I'd heard, was at the opposite end of the spectrum. Located in Kenai Country, where the number of drift boats can resemble the Spanish Armada and the little riverside towns swell to ten times their normal size during summer, Quartz is one of the go-tos for walk-and-wade anglers. Granted, it's a dandy fishery with trophy-sized trout and dollies sulking around its pools, but I'd seen enough photos of fish with deformed jaws and similar grotesque evidence of roadside catch-and-release to turn me off to the whole thing.

First, I stopped along the upper stretches, though I didn't catch anything and came upon some gypsy camp where shotguns were blasting like fireworks and I left before I became a homicide victim. I drove down to the mouth, which is also part of a popular campground, and turned right back around when I saw about six people fishing the same run. I ended up fishing a stretch about a mile or so up from the mouth, right off the highway but where there was only one other car parked.

The creek looked and smelled fishy. I tied on a flesh pattern and worked my way down, passing a pair of anglers on the opposite bank who drilled glares at me through their polarizers. They had Kenai Brewing hats on and looked like they knew what they were doing. I found a suitable place to cross and, not expecting much, started fishing myself. No sooner had I made a few casts than the pair of anglers came up behind me.

Clearly waiting for me to leave, they assumed classic 'smoke 'em if you got 'em' stances, and one of them even went as far as whittling a stick. Unfortunately for them, I'd since decided that they were locals, and when locals give you dirty looks and refuse to jump around you and the pool you're fishing, you've gotta think you're onto something. More than that, I could see a pair of nice rainbows noodling around in the wake of a leaning tree, along with a mammoth-sized dolly who was glued to the bottom and proved uninterested in looking at flies. Both rainbows, though, surprised the hell out of me when I hooked them. One got away after leaping a few times, and the other made it into the net and I held his fat silvery body for a moment before letting him go. He was a real roadside gem; all of sixteen inches, colors bright as the eyes of a lapidary, for all I knew a virgin flying below radar in this creek pummeled by boot tracks.

I looked up and the other guys were gone. I fished down a little way farther and came upon a merganser sleeping on a gravel bar. Not wanting to wake him, I turned around and headed back upstream.

# SIXTEEN: GULKANA AGAIN

A T SOME POINT BETWEEN NINE P.M. AND FIVE A.M., I'm think-ing less about how cold it is both inside and outside the tent and more about the fact that I'd conned Emmie into hiking six miles through swamp (twelve if you consider the trip *back*) all for one little rainbow trout that barely scraped twelve inches. This is sometimes how things go for me—rarely as planned, sometimes poorly enough to be considered 'debacles' or 'follies'—though I usually face the consequences alone. Listening to Emmie whimper and shiver right next to me makes me feel about as low as a guy can because, no doubt about it, this is my fault. That and her worst nightmare takes shape in the form of a vole rooting through our trash bag at around midnight.

At five-thirty I get up and heat up a water bottle and put it into her sleeping bag, then I gather sticks by the thin beam of a head-lamp and get a fire going. There's not much to do other than gather more wood and stand there in the dark listening to the canyon.

Two days before, I was chasing grouse with Emmie's husky named Rowdy, a dog who, drama aside, is the toughest animal

I've ever crossed paths with. That dog has fought tooth-and-nail with coyotes, wolves, bears, and God knows what else for going on twelve years. He no longer has teeth, he can barely hear anything short of a 12-gauge fired next to his ear, and his entire face is whittled with scars.

Rowdy and I didn't get anything, so I started packing the backpacks that Emmie and I would be toting for our upcoming expedition. A certain fly-fishing publication had expressed interest in running an article about the Gulkana River and its population of rainbow trout and steelhead, which have been defined as one of the northernmost populations in the world. Being an impatient and amateur photographer, my last trip to try and catch these fish hadn't produced many pictures suitable for a magazine, so it seemed that a second expedition would be required to further flesh out my own profile of the river. It took all of two seconds for me to think, *Why don't I bring my professional photographer wife along*? She spends her summer weekends chasing brides and grooms around and taking some truly epic photos of their weddings. I don't even know nor care about half of these people but Emmie's pictures have a way of making you want to.

Let me say for the record that she *volunteered* to go on the trip before I even asked her. I knew just how exhausting and endless the hike was from my previous experience in July. Emmie was physically capable and tough enough to handle it, of course, but for what? I could get pretty sappy about the support she has for me and my reckless writing and fishing hobbies, but the fact of the matter is that Emmie is just one of those amazing women that only come along a few times in their generation; completely selfless, completely kind, completely the best companion a fellow could ever ask for, and one that I don't deserve in the least. Sometimes I wonder why she chose me and how she could've seen past the boy-band hair and self-obsessed reek of my sixteenth year, but that can quickly become as pointless as trying to answer any of the other 'big' questions in life. Usually, I've found, it's best just to shut up and enjoy it.

The morning of our trek, we were up in the frosted dark of early September listening to the coffeemaker wheeze and oil writhe around the fry pan. I won't say we were in a hurry, but I wanted to get to the trailhead at dawn. During my trips to and from the truck I made sure to rub Rowdy's neck. No one is ever too busy to stop and pet a good dog.

The Haggard Creek trail turned out to be as bad as it was in July, with the bonus that most of the water we had to slog through was glazed over in ice that crackled and bit at our shins. We'd steeled ourselves for the misery, but even stoicism can wear thin after a while.

Blueberries and rosehips hung shriveled and the land was awash in autumn color. We talked about the world and what a crazy year 2020 had turned out to be, and when we bushwhacked off the trail we wondered if we were the first people to set foot in some of those places. Emmie had once worked for the Bureau of Land Management and the National Park Service, both of which like to get out and conduct archaeological surveys in the summer, so she said probably not. Beyond the Athabascan people that have lived here for thousands of years, some intern from Connecticut had probably dug up a potsherd right where we stomped. You never know, though, and this land is big.

FOR ME, FISHING IS A LOT OF GRAPPLING WITH the astronomical odds of hooking something at all. I'm not especially perceptive to the habits of fish, I don't possess encyclopedic knowledge of rivers and where trout hold, I'm not skilled at thinking outside the box, and sometimes I overthink things to the point that the sheer improbability of catching fish against the heavy weight of cynicism beats me into a kind of submission that likes to sit in camp and pout. The only real things I can say I've got going for myself are that A.) Sometimes I get lucky, and (B.) I'm stupid enough to hike twelve miles through swamp to catch a twelve-inch trout and not be entirely disappointed about that.

That's how it ended up going. I brought one twelve-inch rainbow to hand, granted a twelve-inch rainbow that was among the wildest and northernmost on the planet. I hooked a few others, one that even got my heart rollicking when I felt his weight and saw a flash of silver the size of a basketball, but that's how it goes.

Now that I think about it, there might even be more beauty in not catching a fish than in catching one. I'm of the belief that fishing is one of the few things in life where output is truly correlated with effort—that whole "you get out of it what you put into it" mantra that Dad always harps about. Moreover, the more strenuous or unpleasant the effort, the more significant the reward. I like to think that I'm basically caching into a savings account every time I do something stupid like tackling the Haggard Creek trail, and I do it in the belief that someday I can redeem my coffers for something like a thirty-five-inch Gulkana steelhead.

Beyond that, sometimes it's just fun to do something crazy and foolish and pointless, at least in the outdoor sports department. It's kind of my own way of flipping the bird to a world that sees fishing as a joke and an excuse to drink cheap beer.

The canyon was more beautiful than I remembered it being, probably because the sheer rocks were caught in angular fall sunlight and the rest of it was sharp and vital with the colors of death. We made camp up above the rafting portage trail, and while I plied casts through the rapids, Emmie read and took a nap. Dinner was simple and pathetic; a bag of packaged spaghetti that was calorically enough to satisfy a housecat. I fished until the sun was buried and we settled in for one of the coldest nights in my living memory. I'll spare you the monotony by saying only that Emmie and I, while sitting around the campfire the next morning in a listless daze, decided we'd buy subzero sleeping bags as soon as we were back in town.

As the sun rose and the land warmed, squirrels chattered about their to-do lists. Gray jays, the masked camp bandits, squabbled aimlessly when they realized we had no trash to rob.

Everything seemed restless, like campers too cold to sleep, like a tangle of life when there's so much to do that you do nothing at all. Soon the entire place will freeze solid. Snow will fall, stick, and bury; marten and ermine tracks will crisscross the country. Ravens will croak from the tip-tops of spruce trees, and in a vast stadium of forty-below the sound will echo for miles.

A fleeting part of me longs for those dark days, for stalking the winter ghosts of snowshoe hares, for the quiet fireside afternoons spent tying flies and planning the next summer.

The thoughts melt when the sun finally clears the trees, and I feel warmth and possibility for the last few weeks of open water. It ain't over yet. Emmie and I sip coffee and plan our next few weekends, then we saddle up and guess the direction of the highway.

# SEVENTEEN: SISYPHUS AND STEELHEAD

E MMIE'S GOT A REASONABLE-ENOUGH RESPONSE when I tell her my weekend plan:
"Who is this guy again?"

Normally, a question like that might precede a cryptic business arrangement, or worse, my own kidnapping, but the guy's a hardcore fly angler named Andy, so how bad can he be? I tell Emmie as much. Andy is a research geneticist that I met through recording a hunting podcast at work back in March 2020. He came on as a guest to talk about zoonotic diseases—a very timely subject if you'll recall those days. Through exchanged emails, I knew Andy had recently been to Tierra Del Fuego to fish for giant sea-run brown trout and had also chased Alaskan steelhead with impressive success. Months later, I also knew that when someone like that asks you to go steelhead fishing, you do it. Skip work if you have to

The brief from Andy was that we'd spend three days fishing hard for steelhead and cohos on the Kenai Peninsula, namely in the famed Anchor River, Deep Creek, and one other stream with a similarly large steel run but with a befuddling lack of fishing pressure. We'd camp in nearby parking lots so that we could fish from sun-up to sun-down, but if it got too cold, Andy said, we could get a room at some dingy place like the Anchor River Inn.

I'd had plans to chase rainbow trout farther north, but I didn't really think twice about rearranging my weekend. I'd never caught a steelhead before and figured I ought to if I wanted to carry any sort of clout in a fly-fishing conversation.

The fish themselves are a tough one to peg for me. I understand the cult status that steelhead have achieved in the fly-fishing world, with a membership that will quit their jobs, abandon their spouses (the few that have them in the first place), and live like vagabonds while chasing a fish that comes along about once in every thousand casts. Steelhead are a handsome fish to be sure, either fresh from the sea and sterling-bright or dolled up in sanguine watercolors of the spawn, and the fact that they are trout commonly going north of thirty-five inches sounds like a mutation of nature. Part of their draw, too, is fishing the quintessential Pacific Northwestern rivers where they are found, muscling flies and sink-tips endlessly into the flow, losing a heartbreakingly large number of the few you actually hook. I *get* it; though having come from a state that's about as far from a coastal stream as you can get, and having been content to fish for smaller (and more agreeable) trout on skinnier water most of my life, I've rarely *done* it.

I showed up at Andy's house at around seven on a Friday morning. He and his wife, Lili, live up above the city where they have a view that unluckier folks might pay by the night for. The sun was high enough to put Denali, two hundred miles north, in a limelight of alpenglow. Out across the ocean, calm and lonely, the white teeth of mountains rose. Andy and I loaded up his truck in the wordless, anticipatory daze that hovers before fishing trips, then we were heading south toward the Kenai Peninsula as conversation grew.

Among the topics covered were the inevitable coronavirus, his research on wildlife diseases, my trajectory through a wildlife degree, a video producer gig, and now a teaching certificate, how we both came to Alaska in the first place, our favorite flies, and fishing internationally. I played listener for most of these since I haven't fished internationally before (unless you count a tiny free-stone creek in northern British Columbia). Andy, on the other hand, is a veteran. He'd been to Uruguay for golden dorado, where he'd also been pitched out of a boat into a set of not-insignificant rapids (which he obviously survived); he'd been to Jurassic Lake in Argentina (twice!), which has become something of a fly-fishing Mecca for unfathomably large rainbow trout; he'd chased bone-fish in Venezuela; tarpon in Belize; browns in Tierra Del Fuego; and, in Alaska specifically, he'd tangled with huge Dolly Varden and sheefish in the far reaches of the Arctic. I'm sure he got sick of my questions, but it was about all I could do to avoid fan-boying him to death.

In Soldotna we stop for a few groceries and a box of assorted IPAs, then it's back to the mission at hand. By then it's eleven in the morning and you'd be hard-pressed to find a more beautiful day in this country. Not a cloud in the sky, the atmosphere as blue as the belly of a Steller's jay, the conical ghosts of Mount Redoubt and Iliamna, both active volcanoes, throbbing in the heat.

We pass a series of steelhead streams, which have progres-sively larger runs the further south you go, and make rough plans for how we'll fish them in the coming days. Our next stop is the Anchor River, at a campground tucked off the main highway and reached only by crossing a wonderfully bucolic little truss bridge. I swear that if you find an old fly-fishing calendar and flip to a month like September or October, you'll see what I saw. A pair of fishermen stood in a hole below the bridge—a hole that Andy assured me is good for a steelhead or two on most days—making casts against a stage of deciduous fire. I couldn't help but think that as much as I seek solitude and have come to grumble about crowds on the river, this was one of those magic times where the pool would've seemed far too lonely had it been empty. We parked and those same two fishermen waddled back to their truck for lunch, where we found out that the fishing was slow, but that the steelhead were around.

I can say we gave the Anchor an honest try, fishing down from the bridge a full mile-and-a-half or so to its mouth in the Cook Inlet. It's called the Anchor after one of Captain James Cook's expeditions here in 1778, when his *HMS Resolution* battled a violent north wind and eventually lost their anchor. I can't help but wonder if it's still down there. We pass a few anglers en route, one of which professed that he'd caught a few steelhead before taking a break to call his wife (and either tell her the good news or swear he'd be home soon). Andy and I never experienced such luck, so we returned to the campground to devise our next move.

Back at the truck, there was a talkative guy with a salt-and-pepper mustache holding a Modelo in one hand and his phone in the other, showing any and all that would give him the time of day a photo of a steelhead he'd caught that morning. At first, he told us there was no way he was giving up the location, but he must've had a good buzz going because minutes later he did just that. We had to extract ourselves before he really got going—you gotta be wary of a steelheader that talks too much.

At a fly shop just up the road (the self-proclaimed "Most Westerly Fly Shop in North America," and the only one for miles), we ask the guy if he's got any firewood. He says no, but that there's a pile of it just up the road for ten bucks a bundle. He goes on to tell us that the steelhead fishing is picking up. I find out later that this same bloke keeps an online blog about the fishing, and his updates, more so than anything else, contribute to the ebb and flow of crowds on the Peninsula streams. Fish and Game just installed a counting weir specifically for steelhead, too, so now people have actual numbers to look at. Theoretically, it takes the guesswork out of timing the steelhead run, but also makes it that much harder to beat the crowds. Just up the road, we buy firewood on the honor system and come to find out later that it's way too wet.

At Deep Creek we pitched a spartan camp and fished our way downstream toward the sunset. Aside from a few dollies that Andy hooked, things were quiet. We came back in the dark and cracked into our box of IPAs and cooked hot dogs on sticks before calling it a day. A blue van pulled up and its driver, a young gun with a full, blonde beard, asked us how the fishing was. We said the usual something like, "Fishin' was slow, but it was a beautiful day."

There was a good chance there would be frost in the morning.

THE LEGEND OF SISYPHUS IS ONE that should be well-known by now, if only because it demonstrates that consequences come with deceit, and that sometimes humans will slave themselves toward ends that don't really make sense. In Greek mythology, Sisyphus was the king of an ancient metropolis. He routinely killed travelers to secure his place on the throne, he plotted the killing of his brother (coincidentally named Salmoneus), and he, more than once, cheated death and his assigned tenure in the Underworld. In modern America, Sisyphus would be something like a fraudulent CEO or a tax evader—maybe a few select politicians, too, but like I always say, that kind of talk isn't welcome on the water. There was an instance where Death itself was ordered by Zeus to chain Sisyphus below the Underworld, though Sisyphus tricked Death into showing him how the chains worked and chained Death there instead.

In any case, it was Zeus that got the last laugh by eventually getting his hands around the slippery Sisyphus and cursing him to an eternity worse than death: rolling a boulder up a mountain, over and over again without the ability to cease or die. Every time Sisyphus neared the peak with his onerous load, the boulder would roll back down to the bottom and he'd have to start from the beginning.

I doubt I was thinking about Sisyphus that morning. Andy and I followed the blue wedges of headlamps down to a hole near Deep Creek's mouth, where we drifted an endless procession of casts and occasionally stopped to blow on our hands and inject some feeling back into our fingers. It was cold, all right. Somewhere in the waking world I heard the cackle of a rooster pheasant, a sound which I hadn't heard since leaving Wyoming six years before. Apparently, someone was raising them along the highway. Dawn came on about as spectacular as you could ever want, the gray curtains folding back to gold and pink, the sun trickling over spruce tops, the cold making things feel righteous and proper.

We didn't catch a steelhead, but we watched a guy do it. We were coming back upstream, and by then the holes below the bridge were taken up by a trio of be-wadered and be-jacketed fishermen. One, in particular, was fishing a good-looking run with a little Spey rod, and just as we passed, he hooked up to a good fish. Andy offered to net it for him, but the man seemed as unamused by that as he did by us standing and watching, so he played his fish downstream around the next bend and out of sight. Good for him, we thought. At least he wasn't parading the fish to all and sundry like Modelo man.

Over coffee and scones we plotted our next move. Anchor and Deep Creek would be overrun being that it was a Saturday (and being that the most Westerly fly shop had updated its blog with encouraging reports), but Andy had an inkling about a stream farther north. Upon mutual agreement we leapt to it and dismantled camp.

I DON'T HAVE MUCH EXPERIENCE FLOATING RIVERS—IN FACT, I can count the number of times I've floated anything on one hand—so it was lucky that Andy did. He owns a beast of a raft that's seen more waters than he can reasonably count, he's smooth on the oars, or "the sticks" as he calls them, and he approaches the whole thing with a casual amusement that instills unflappable confidence in his passengers. Unlike me, he's not worried about the rapids ahead, or if the vehicle shuttle will work out, or how many other boats could be below us. He's just a fellow chasing steelhead, again, on secret water.

It was mid-morning when we landed on the first gravel bar. Andy had brought his Spey rod and stood piecing it together while I threaded line through the guides of my single-hander. Salmon littered the shore like the aftermath of a trench fight, and soon I was making casts, swinging flies, and moving up and down the bank between the carcasses. Before long, Andy was casting too, whipping out flights of fly line that just seemed to keep going and going like baseballs soaring over a centerfield fence. We fell into a rhythm of fishing downstream to the end of the run, always equally spaced, then we'd go back to the top and start all over.

"How many steelhead you land?" we'd sometimes ask as we passed.

If only.

I had to wonder what a steelhead would feel like. I figured I had to be getting close to the thousand-cast mark, and when you start seeing them as a quantity, those casts can become as emotionless and mechanical as the movements of a serial killer. I started imagining shoving a boulder up a mountain, first one time, then two, then I lost count at seven. Rolling and casting alike began to seem equally laborious and equally functionless; something a kid would do on his Saturday afternoon because his dad encouraged him to under the guise that it would "build character" but stretched to the point of mild insanity.

I don't need to tell anybody that when you start feeling discouraged like that is usually about the time you hook a fish. I recall I was fishing up near where someone had once hung a clothesline in the trees, and on the swing before I'd felt a knock that I'd dismissed as a rock. On the second pass, something latched onto the hook and squirreled out a few feet of line, but before I could really get a gauge on its size, it was gone.

Other people have lost fish. People since the beginning of time have lost fish, and even though the feeling is as universal as stubbing your toe, you always feel like you're the only one.

The day passed in parabolas; waves, the loops of eagles, the dances of graphite, the slow tumble of daylight. We fished several runs that looked good, but the river wasn't giving up any secrets. I could start to see how steelheading is as much the casting and the water as it is the fish, for the same reason that bass fishermen only talk about the weather and the sunset when the fishing is slow. Andy and I would pass by each other and offer small grins, or we'd say things like, "No one can say we ain't tryin.'" Our heads would jolt at every sound of fly line being yanked off the water, every rogue splash, but these were only rocks, foul-hooked pink salmon, or new casts.

My first steelhead came about as unceremoniously as it could have. I was fishing a bead pegged above a flesh fly, in fact, targeting dollies more than anything else, and combing it through some slack water down below the main run. I must've dozed off on my feet because when I came to, the indicator was gone.

It was a fish I never should have caught, a total fluke, and when Andy saw my rod dipping, he ran to get the net. It turned out to be only a small steelhead, smaller than my largest resident rainbow, but she was bright as a silver vein and zoomed out of my hands like a supercar when it came time to release her. Andy might have been more jazzed than I was. Prior to catching her, I thought getting my hands on just one steelhead might be enough; that these hours, these days of rolling boulders and rolling casts would be suddenly validated. I'd have caught the fish of a thousand casts, meaning I'd *made* those thousand casts and secured my place in some angling pantheon of raw grit, and I could move on. Looking back, though, the opposite happened.

THAT NIGHT WE CAMPED NEARBY, and we knew we were in the right place as soon as we saw a familiar blue van parked in the middle of the road. It was the blonde-bearded chap we'd run into the night before, only this time he was staring up into the trees, his knuckles white against a chunk of firewood.

"You guys mind pullin' forward?" he asked as we stopped. "There's a spruce hen up in the tree." Apparently, he needed some dinner.

Moments later the firewood launched from one sinewy arm and he came up to our window, eyes wide as though he'd just escaped an asylum.

"Missed her. How'd you guys do floating?"

We told him, to which he replied that he'd lost a mid-thirties fish that afternoon. He didn't say where, but he went on to tell us that we wouldn't have much luck fishing this lower section. Andy and I decided that we'd give it a try in the morning anyway, but that tonight we just wanted to commemorate a fish with two bottles of beer. We set up camp and clinked to chrome.

Somewhere within earshot of the campsite, a diligent hound started barking at around nightfall and didn't let up until well into the next morning. I'm not sure what had him so upset, but Andy and I agreed that the register of his wails put him in either the Rottweiler or the Newfoundland category.

Just before we went to bed, and just after the howls of the mutt were joined by a far-off, jovial cheering, the bearded guy slunk into our camp with his fishing partner. Turns out, they'd been whooping and hollering down on the river because they landed a few thirty inchers and doubled up on feisty cohos. So much for the lower river not being worth fishing. He introduced himself as Luke, or alternatively, "the weird guy with the van," which seemed far more appropriate, and his buddy was called John. They both looked like the types who had spent most of their lives in waders and logged more fishing hours than I did, which is always a trait I deeply respect if not envy. Luke was a guide who'd grown up on the Kenai, and John was a California steelheader who was bumming around the Peninsula on his way to see his fiancé in Anchorage. His occupation was a little more clandestine, though he said something about Uber and weed, and not the kind that grows in ditches. Andy and I would discuss it at some length later and decide that, all things considered, it just might be legitimate. That night we chewed the fat with the pair of 'em until we scattered off to bed, all fully aware that the only people to beat to the water in the morning were each other.

I fell asleep wondering if I had what it took to be a serious fisherman—that is, the caliber of Andy, Luke, and John, the steelhead apostles who knew the thrill of big trout and chased it with no questions asked. I wondered if I could keep rolling the boulder for weekends on end, even as the nights got colder and colder and the mornings darker and darker.

It was two weeks later that I got my next crack at a steelhead.

Andy had gone down with another buddy to the Anchor the weekend before and had enjoyed an absolutely cosmic few days of fishing; 'cosmic' here meaning thirteen steelhead and bright sunny skies and more or less complete solitude. The kind of weekend that you only get once every decade, basically; the kind of weekend that had me a little green with jealousy considering I spent mine drenched with rain and repairing a flat tire on the Denali Highway. No matter; Andy invited me down that next Friday and, though we both figured it best to appease our wives on Sunday, we planned to fish hard for two days.

My eight-weight reel had been slowly deteriorating, and I could've gotten sentimental about the chips in the nickel plating or the gravelly creak of the drag, but I didn't. It was one of the first fly reels I ever bought, and a kid can be hard on stuff when he doesn't know what he's doing. I bought a new one the Thursday before we left and didn't look back.

The Anchor was looking dismal for our trip. The same rain that washed me out on a creek farther north had been dumping on the Kenai Peninsula, and water levels were almost double what they'd been the weekend before. We opted for the lesser known stream and said a few Hail Marys. Who was waiting in the parking lot but a familiar, blue van. I half-expected a brace of spruce grouse to be hanging from a side mirror. The Rottweiler was wailing again, too.

Luke and John had been at it for a few days already, we'd come to find out. They claimed a slow weekend prior and a few hookups that day. The one reality they voiced, and one the persistent rain would come to confirm, was that the water was comin' up. I knew steelhead only insofar as Andy had conveyed during our now four days fishing together, but I knew rising water was bad. Sure, it could bring more steelhead in on the tides, but it dirtied the river like creamer dumped in coffee and for whatever reason—one that I'm convinced borders on the supernatural—the fish just turned off. We fished until dark that night, drifting ten-millimeter beads that Andy and I had scrupulously picked from a collection at a fly shop in Cooper Landing. We each hooked a Dolly and watched mergansers skate overhead, then we had to call it a night because we could barely see our indicators, let alone the trail back to the truck. Luke and John had staggered off into the night well before that, and I haven't seen either of them since.

We got McDonald's in town because everything else had closed at eight, which is as sure a sign that you're staring down the barrel of winter as any. Andy and I are both thin fellows despite our tendencies to eat complete junk on fishing trips and we talk about this at some length while we sit in the drive-through. The conversation only diverts when we start commenting on the truck in front of us, which was one of those old beaters with duct tape on the taillights and the general appearance of a vehicle that recently went head-to-head with a rhinoceros. I bet it had a valiant heater in it, though.

I can't say I've ever stayed in a hotel room on a fishing trip. Luckily, Andy had, so he knew the dividends that sleeping in a comfortable bed and waking up in an environment that wasn't a frosted-over tent could pay while on the water. We got to our room and watched a few sports highlights before hitting the proverbial hay, which I have to say was much nicer than layering up with jackets and shaking myself into a sleeping bag and hoping my wader boot laces didn't freeze to the point that I couldn't tie them in the morning.

I HAD TO WONDER (AGAIN) IF I'D EVER SEE A STEELHEAD—that is, a steelhead that was properly steelhead-sized and not a total accident. I'm not entirely superstitious—though I *have* been known to set my alarm to only even-numbered times and I refuse to replace my fishing hat—but that can be tough to avoid in situations like this. Steelhead just have that air about them. And when you *know* there are steelhead around and you've *seen* other folks catch them in the same places you've fished, you've gotta start wondering about things. At least Sisyphus *knew* he was working toward nothing; I don't have the luxury of that distinction. I'm working toward a thought, my casts and weekends a series of means to an end, and that end is a pendulous tumble into a repeatable cycle; an infinite loop of getting closer and closer but never actually reaching the mountaintop.

Morning rescued me. Both Andy and I had alarms set for around six, but we were up and having coffee by 5:30. Emmie had made cinnamon rolls which constituted breakfast. Outside the stars were poking through inky sky and some teenagers were sharing a joint.

We were the first ones to the river, and I won't say we rushed to get rigged up, but we didn't dawdle either. Soon we were back in default position, which was thigh-deep in a long run, watching glow-in-the-dark indicators shimmy like rubber ducks across an unknown surface.

"Things feel fishy this morning," I told Andy, and I meant it. The air had that grimy stickiness to it that I'd felt on some of the best days of my summer; the first of the Klutina sockeyes, my biggest Gulkana rainbow, the procession of mayfly hatches and rising grayling up on the Clearwater. Those days felt about as far away as Pluto, but like a coho or a steelhead returning to its natal stream, I could recall exactly how the air smelled, tasted, and pressed against my jacket. I thought that of all the days I'd spent whipping casts for steelhead and questioning every pattern in my fly boxes, this was going to be the one. There would be that one time the indicator dipped and it *wasn't* a branch and I'd yank the rod downstream and I'd feel something come back in the form of electricity.

I never got that feeling that day, but I fished all morning in a buzz of hope as palpable as steam rising from a cooked hot dog. A new, good friend was making pretty casts just upstream of me, a pair of trumpeter swans lumbered overhead like cargo planes, and I started to understand that noticing stuff like that wasn't because we weren't catching fish. It felt like the world was rewarding us for trying.

# EIGHTEEN: DUCK DAYS

After letting a weekend elapse where I did no fishing whatsoever, you could say I was itching to give it one last go before winter set in for good. My bones craved the signature of a fly rod: the featherlight heft, the lively flex, the casual but precise flight of line. It felt a lot like springtime in this regard, though the unfortunate reality was that summer was behind me and I had six months ahead of more cravings that I could do nothing about. Fall was underway and winter was near, so near that at night, if you listened beyond the angst of the city, you could hear the clamor of Canadian geese headed south.

It would remind me of growing up in Wyoming; listening to the sandhill cranes and the geese and the mallards rustle overhead, smelling the clean break between wintery air and woodsmoke. Fall was my season then just as now, a long list of to-dos and want-to-dos that leeched over into distracting me from school.

It's impressive just how quickly Alaska shuts down once summer is over. I don't know if all the diners and campgrounds and B&Bs convene at some point and decide "We close *today*," or if it's just coincidence, but when one is boarded up and the windows are dark, they all are. For year-round residents like myself, this usually stirs questions like, "Well where am I supposed to eat *now*?" Luckily, the gas stations stay open, at least.

The campground I normally park at to fish from is guarded by barrels. The first time this happened, a couple of years ago, I was brazen enough to weasel my truck past them. When my buddy Ryan Kelly and I had finished fishing for the day we returned to find a note on the windshield.

*Don't drive past barrels*, it said. *Your license plate number has been sent to troopers.*

That might have worried me if it hadn't been worth it, but that was one of the best days of trout fishing I've ever had. I figured I'd tell the troopers that when they called. They never did.

This time I don't go around the barrels—the campground manager and I have an agreement—but instead park up the road and walk down to the bridge. It's a brisk day with the flattened grays of overcast sky, one I don't mind walking in if only to warm up before I proceed to stand heron-still in the water.

It takes me a while to find the trout because the water is so low. Years ago, Ryan and I stood hip-deep catching sixteen-to-twenty-two-inch trout for hours in a stretch no more than a hundred yards long. Now that same run is a gravel bar. The first fish I stick fights about as sluggishly as he must feel, though he manages to throw the hook right at the bank. The next fish I hook feels huge, and I mean *huge*. I've heard stories of ten-pound rainbows here (it is Alaska, after all), but with how much pressure this creek gets you never really believe that. Now I'm convinced I've hooked one of these brutes, so you can imagine my disappointment when I find out it was a twenty-incher hooked just behind the dorsal. Oh well. It was a pretty fish.

With enough light left to drive north and poke around for some grouse, I walk back to the truck. Water freezes on my rod guides. I go through the campground, past the boarded outhouses and the gray emptiness of vacant picnic tables. Near the barrels and the sign that says "Campground CLOSED", I find a perfect ruffed grouse feather.

I THINK EVERYONE SHOULD EXPERIENCE their favorite trout stream without having any intentions of fishing it—at least once. Admittedly, this was the first time I came down into my particular creek bottom wearing anything but waders. The heft of a shotgun instead of a fly rod felt bizarre.

At the first beaver slough I come to I spook a good flock of mallards. I draw on them with the safety on just for the practice of mounting the gun, then I think about running to buy a duck stamp for the next day. Duck hunting isn't something I've done much of in the past, at least not seriously. The thought of sitting in front of a decoy spread and freezing my tail off has yet to become appealing, and my jump-shooting escapades as a teenager in Wyoming proved I was better suited for trapping mink or fishing for creek chubs. I don't think I ever managed to shoot one. Now that I *really* think about it, I know I didn't.

I follow along the creek for a while, wondering if the trout are still here or if they've already high-tailed it into the main river. I realize that I should have worn waders when I go to cross—a little water spills over my boot tops, but I make it okay. The opposite side looks like grouse city, but in a half hour of zigzagging through birch and high-bush cranberries I kick up none. I use a log crossing and head back to the truck just as the sun starts going down.

Tomorrow I'll start out with the fly rod and fish downstream to the mouth. I'll have the shotgun in tow, so I'll try jumping a few ducks on the way back up. What's twenty-five bucks for a stamp, anyway?

I'm imagining the pneumatic wings of erupting fowl, the moment of slowness just before they reach full speed. I may not have ever shot a duck, but I've spooked enough to know that the chaos of duck-flight, the whistle of primaries, the silhouettes of birds in a sunset sky are as essential to the heart of an outdoorsman as a grouse flushing, a deer materializing, a trout rising. I forget about all of that when I come out on the highway and see the car on fire.

DAYS ARE DAYS.

John Denver called some of them diamonds and some of them stones. For me it was a "hooked three trout, landed one at twenty-one inches" kind of day (as 'diamond' as any). But for the owner of that burning car—and I honestly don't remember her name because she was so plastered that she couldn't, either—it was a new contender for worst day of her life. As it should've been. She'd drifted across the road and smashed a guardrail head-on.

By the time I came along, another vehicle had pulled over and a couple was helping the woman out of the smoldering wreckage. To the woman this was an inconvenience; ten more minutes and she could've nursed that nice warm buzz forever.

I parked on the side of the road just as the couple, who I later learned were named Jeremy and Stephanie and were lovely people, was setting the woman down and swaddling her in a blanket. The woman was old, with sallow skin and thinning hair, and she had this blank smile on her face like she knew she was screwed but was enjoying herself anyway. She had one scratch on her forehead. At her feet were the only two items that she thought to grab from the car; a chunk of foam and a brown paper bag the exact size and shape of a fifth of whiskey. Other cars soon stopped, as well, and I started to think there were a little too many cooks in the kitchen and that I had better things to do than watch an intoxicated old bird try and blabber out her own name. Those other cars soon had the same idea, though, and disappeared.

Eventually, Jeremy, Stephanie, myself, and some other guy with a fire extinguisher decided that it was colder than a witch's mammary and carried the woman up to sit in a warm vehicle. God forbid she get hypothermia. Of course, the only vehicle with space in the passenger seat was mine.

While the others kept talking to the woman in loud voices to keep her from passing out, I was watching her through the windshield with narrowed eyes and feeling a mix of pity and hate. Mostly I was watching to make sure she didn't puke on my dashboard or steal anything. She'd since demonstrated her lack of courtesy. What if someone had been driving the other way? What if that someone had been a family—two kids, say five and six, a mother with a nice face and a habit of delivering homemade relish to neighbors around the holidays, a father who liked duck hunting on the weekends. What if that someone had been my wife? My cheeks tighten like fists and I start wishing they hadn't pulled the woman out. I start thinking, *Go ahead, lady, do something stupid. Give me a reason to fetch the shotgun from the backseat.*

Looking back, I wish I'd gone down and grabbed the whiskey bottle from out of the ditch. I wish I'd brought it up to the truck and shoved it in her face and told her the obvious, so loudly and so clearly that it would've penetrated even her witless dome: "You're screwed, you old hag. *You. Are. Screwed.*"

The ambulance finally showed up about an hour later. They dropped her on a stretcher and drove away. I was outta there, too.

I spent a fitful night in the back of my truck, not because I was thinking about the woman, but because I couldn't stretch my legs past a ninety-degree angle and because, like I said, it was colder than a witch's mammary out there. It wouldn't get light until eight or so, but I was up at four-thirty. I let the truck idle for a while as I made a cup of coffee, then I killed the engine and basked in the warmth as it leaked skyward. As soon as the gas station opened, I went in and bought my duck stamp.

When the sun finally rises, it does so slowly. Alaska is the land of winter for half the year and long sunrises for the other. I start wading the creek in what you'd call civil twilight. Being that the shotgun is strapped to my backpack, and I'm armed with only a six-weight, I naturally spook up a good pod of mallards right off the bat.

I can feel the season fading as I go downstream. The sun rises in its own sweet time, glowing bright as a blowtorch, but the air is irreversibly frigid, and the pools are empty. I follow the water's direction, growing drowsy and eerily content like someone in the clutches of hypothermia. It was a good summer, studded with the images of sockeyes on early June mornings, grayling rising to hatches, patient rainbows in impossible places, lake trout and steelhead that should've, could've, would've worked out, but didn't. I carry all of them with the water, the weight of miles and all the tire rubber I've spent since April digging into my shoulders. Emmie and I have lived in three homes since then.

There are some of those days I wish I could have back. Some decisions I'd not make and others I would. You know how it is. The creek is pensive. I think about how worried I was to give up my cushy job and start interning as a teacher; the fever of beginning, the exhaustion of riding it out like a saddle bronc. Come Monday it'll all be back.

I STARTED THE SEASON TIPTOEING ACROSS DEAD BROME to have a look at some trumpeter swans in my father-in-law's hayfield; I'll end it staring at my boots on a gravel bar, hoping pathetically that the pintail doesn't take wing just yet. She's resting in a little slough where Ryan once caught a twenty-three-inch trout, and with some similar luck, I'll be able to cook her with some wild cranberry sauce. With each step, slow as honey drizzle, I run through all the wing shooting advice I've ever heard. *Mount the gun like you mean it,* Dad would say. *Keep your head down. Don't think.*

Dad was a devoted duck hunter in his early years, though once my brother and I came along his days afield became preciously rare. My childhood was spent in the company of Labrador Retrievers; Zeke, Annie, Chip, Molly, and Doc, all vestiges of Dad's craving for duck blinds that hadn't really gone away. When we moved to Wyoming, and the mallards would whistle through the winter skies, thousands of them, you would sometimes see Dad stop on his way in from chores and just stare up at them. Then he'd grab another armful of firewood and come inside and say something about building a duck blind back on the creek.

We hunted ducks only a few times growing up. Chip, our black Lab, was in his prime at about the same time I was big enough to hold a shotgun by myself. That dog would run himself to death chasing rabbits and four-wheelers, but as soon as you unzipped a gun case he was making a beeline for home. We did end up clearing out a bunch of Russian olive trees back on the creek and throwing them together into a blind like Dad always talked about, though in the fall and winter we were more likely to be trapping raccoons and muskrats than waiting for ducks.

To me it never mattered *which* outdoor pursuit I undertook, though. I think when Dad taught me to love one of them, he taught me to love them all. Just as I yearned for the riseform of a fish or the voltage of checking a string of mink traps, my heart ached for ducks in midflight. On the deep-cold days of winter, I would wander out to Dad's shed and coax the woodstove to life. If I didn't have raccoons to skin (and even if I did), I'd take up my favorite book in Dad's library—his journal—and cozy myself into the moth-eaten recliner. I'd read about Dad's adventures and misadventures of yesteryear, even though I'd read them dozens of times before: the days of fox trapping in the Front Range of Colorado or bagging ducks from creeks that have since been lost to shopping malls. He never specifically told me about the wells of solace you could find out there, or how important all of it could become if you were smart enough to let it, but in those pages, he showed me.

The pintail hen explodes from the water just slightly out of range, and I grit my teeth as I watch her go. Just when I think she's gone, she turns, heads back toward me, quarters away. I throw the gun to my shoulder like I mean it, I keep my head down, I don't think, I don't even register the mule's kick of the gun, and she folds from the sky on the opposite side of the creek.

It was as unceremonious as a hunting pinnacle like that could be; I shared the victory with no one. What used to be a watercourse defined by its good trout holes, or its memorable moments like where Ryan broke his fly rod or where I had the grizzly stand up at me, became something more. I wished I could've carried that duck all the way home, across the alfalfa fields, out past the shed where Dad could look out the kitchen window and see me coming from a long way off. I wished old Chip was alive to see it.

Instead, I skinned and dressed my duck and decided I'd better pick some cranberries to go with it. It was early, I had nowhere to be, and there weren't any fish to catch.

I'VE SINCE TAKEN TO CALLING DAYS like that the 'duck days.' These are the stones that become diamonds, the plans that don't pan out but become something else, something better. Eventually they stack up and form a season—a season just like this one—and then before you know it those seasons pile up to become a life, and one worth remembering.

I got home reasonably early that night, and I took my time unloading the sundries that tend to build up on fishing excursions. I rinsed and packed away my duck in the freezer, pinned her wings out on cardboard either to admire on a wall someday or pluck and use for dry flies, and paced around the kitchen letting the weekend settle into some kind of meaning. Once it did, I sat down on the couch and scribbled it all in my journal with the same kind of shorthand that Dad used to use; succinct, observant, unsentimental, just-another-day while also one of the best days of my life. I suppose I could've filled my pages with sappy love letters to Mother Nature and pseudo-epiphanies about birds, beasts, and fish, but why? It's only hunting, it's only fishing, and what can I pretend to know about it, anyway?

Days later I notice a strange smell in my truck, and it takes me a few seconds to realize what it is. It's the woman's perfume.

JOSEPH JACKSON IS A SOCIAL STUDIES TEACHER by day and a fly
fisherman the rest of the time. If he's not on the water, he's either
pining for it or writing about it. He's been published widely in the
fly-fishing magazine world, where he and his wife, Emmie, also
feature much of their photography. He lives in Anchorage but part
of his heart will always belong to the Wyoming he grew up in. He
was last spotted at a gas station somewhere in the Last Frontier
with a fly rod sticking out the back window. *It's Only Fishing* is his
first book.